PRAISE FOR MY

"Dive into this story when you have plenty of time to swim around in it, because you won't want to come up for air until you've harvested all its pearls."

> ~ DARLYN FINCH KUHN, author of *Red Wax Rose*, *Three Houses*, and *Sewing Holes*

"Read *Pearl* with pen in hand to underline, circle and star. Myra Katherine's effervescence and authenticity in *Pearl* is full of enlightening gems you'll want to resurrect as soon as you turn the next page."

> ~ COURTNEY HUDSON GOODSON, Associate Justice, Arkansas Supreme Court

"Myra Katherine's gift lies in seeing her deeply rooted faith, secure and unwavering even amidst some of life's most adverse seasons, all the while inspiring faith in others. She has a contagious zest for life that is no doubt fueled by her hysterical quick wit and skill in finding humor in all things. Someone who has tasted and seen deep sadness, but exudes the 'deeper still' Godly joy — a living testimony to His goodness."

> ~ RACHEL SCOTT, mother, musician, worship leader

"Myra Katherine's greatest gift to her readers is her honesty. With humor and humility, she shares the stories of her perfectly imperfect life — the heartaches, the frustrations, and the triumphs. So many women experience similar fears and doubts; Myra Katherine gives our struggles a voice and makes us realize we're not alone. Pearl is a true treasure, a collection of her lessons, her revelations, her resilience, and, above all, her faith."

> ~ SUZY MORGAN, English teaching, word loving, single mother of three

"Myra Katherine's writing is honest, real, hilarious, and hopeful. *Pearl* is a book that will encourage readers to keep fighting for the relationships that are closest to them."

> ~ BRIAN STROH, Executive Pastor, Hillcrest Church

"God has not promised us a perfect life in this world, but He does promise to hold us in the storm. May Myra Katherine's words hold you tight as they point us back to Him."

> ~ TARINA STROH, early childhood expert and Children's Education Director at Hillcrest Church

"This is a Christian woman's account of her divorce in a culture that doesn't always welcome divorced Christian women. Myra Katherine understands that we are not offered 'do-overs,' only 'do-betters,' and her experience of recognition that 'we mistakenly believe we must be whole before loving another' is a reminder that we are each broken in our own way. She reminds the reader of the importance of humility and giving thanks while she writes to better understand God's plan for her life."

> ~ MELINDA COULTER TAGGART, Senior Network Process Quality Manager, AT&T

Pearl

Testimonies of faith from a politically liberal,
socially conservative Christian
who dove deep into the ocean and
discovered she could swim

MYRA KATHERINE HALE

PEARL

Published in Fremont, NE, by Rock Hill Publishing.

ISBN-10:0-692-97022-3
ISBN-13:978-0-692-97022-5

Cover Design by:
Cari Rasmussen

Interior Design by:
Brad Kuhn
www.bradkuhnandassociates.com

Author Photo by:
Becky Novacek

CYSTIC FIBROSIS
FOUNDATION
ADDING TOMORROWS

10% of all the profits from the sale of this book will be donated by the author to the Cystic Fibrosis Foundation in honor of her granddaughter, Ella.

Dedication

In memory of my Grandmother Pearl and Mammaw, who were strong women and who raised strong women and whose legacy of broken filters lives on.

To Coulter and Emma Claire: You are my beauty from ashes and my most treasured pearls. For you, I fought for joy. Because of you, I found it.

To my Mother and Daddy: You were right. I was wrong. Thank you for never saying that out loud. At least not where I could hear you. Thank you for keeping me afloat before I learned to swim. I love you the mostest.

To Kimberly: I love you. I love your closet. Thank you for reminding me that I used to sparkle, and for helping me to reclaim my effervescence.

To Gregory: Thank you for loving my children as your own, for sharing your addiction to cows and land, and letting us live this wild, crazy life vicariously through you. You amaze your big sister and we "luuuuv" you.

To Mike: I'm sorry I spoiled your bachelor plans. I'm not really sorry. I am sorry, though, that I'm occasionally strong willed, opinionated and prone to emotional outbursts. Thank you for pretending not to notice. You are my 'restored locust-eating' years, my 'all things worked together for good,' my 'seeing the goodness of the Lord in the land of the living.' Thank you for loving Jesus and leading our family. Being your wife is crazy-fun and I will love you forever.

Acknowledgements

At forty-four, there are many things I've forgotten through the years. The words to the National Anthem (as a soloist in front of an audience of my peers) was probably the most horrifying. I've forgotten to pick up my children from school, but really, what mother hasn't done that? I may have even forgotten to take them on occasion. Ya know, also to school.

It's obviously a deeply psychological issue, because for the past twenty years I've had a reoccurring dream where I get to the end of a college semester only to realize that I've forgotten to attend classes. So this section of acknowledgements is causing me great anxiety. If I can't remember, "Oh, say, can you see ..." how in all of the world am I going to remember to thank everyone who needs thanking?

Tarina: Getting my life back began with your friendship. It began with your honesty and your kind spirit and your love for Jesus. You loved me and you held my hand as I dove. I could not be more grateful.

Jodi: Life is a "both-and." Thank you for teaching me that, showing me that, and living that out loud for all to see. As a stranger you showed me love and grace and compassion and you faithfully pointed me to Christ. My sister and my friend, thank you.

Julie: Thank you for loving me as your daughter and supporting me in all things. With the countless hours we've spent together, there will be no reason for you to read the book. You know the cut and the uncut version and you love me anyway, and for that, thank you!

Janet and Rich: Thank you for taking such good care of us. Pulling weeds; fixing heaters, garage doors, toilets; shoveling snow; actually I can't think of anything you didn't help with!

Suzy: You are a sparkly jewel and literally spread joy. Thank you for the encouragement and early edits.

Jenny: Thank you for your friendship and the many ways you bless us. For hand-me-downs and taco soup and boat rides. P.S. Thanks also for hiding the silver.

Eric: For the plan. It worked, and I am grateful.

Pastor Kyle: Thank you for a door that was always open. For loving me as I ended one life, and pointing me to Christ as I began another.

Melissa: Thank you for covering my children, my marriage, my family in prayer. Your heart for Christ and your gift of mercy has blessed my life. You help me see the world differently, and for that I am grateful.

Tina: I joke about food, but please know that I remember how many times you fed me. Thank you!

Kailey, Dave, Connor, Spencer, and Lucas: I love being part of your family. Thank you for your gracious welcome.

Ella and Isabelle: Mimi loves you. You are adored. We will find a cure and you will slay dragons and if anyone ever tries to hurt you, Mimi will throat-punch them.

Author's Note

"May the words of my mouth and the meditations of my heart be acceptable to you, oh Lord, my strength and my Redeemer."

The pastor of the Methodist Church that I grew up in always began his sermons with this prayer, from the nineteenth Psalm, verse fourteen. According to Joseph Caryl, a prominent minister of the seventeenth century, King David, "could not bear it, that a word, or a thought of his should miss acceptance with God. It did not satisfy him that his actions were well witnessed unto men on earth, unless his very thoughts were witnessed to by the Lord in heaven."

In other words, he (our pastor, not King David) didn't give the first flip if anyone in the congregation found his words acceptable, so long as his Lord did.

So, that's what I'm also saying. I don't care if you like my book.

Okay, I care. A lot.

But be warned. I'm sharing my story. And my story includes exactly five "bad" words. Here they are in order of appearance:

Hell. Shit. Damn. Three variations of the F-word, and Ass.

I use these words with a purpose, not for shock value. Jesus and I have talked about it, and frankly, He's okay with it.

My story also includes sex talk: Having it, not having it, wanting to have it. So Dad, this is probably the only page you should read.

And, for some reason, my story includes this weird dream where we had a President of the United States who wanted to build a wall along our border with Mexico. Oh, wait. That wasn't a dream.

And neither is this.

This is true. This is my story. And my prayer is simply that I will share it in a way that is acceptable in His sight.

Contents

Day One

Friday, October 28, 2016

Driving eight hours from Fremont, Nebraska to Eureka Springs, Arkansas in a rental car (because the "new" car I recently purchased turned out to be a lemon and doesn't, ya know, work) is the shortest road trip that I can remember. I turn on the radio and then quickly shut it off again. All I want is the quiet. I am alone with my thoughts for the first sustained time in years. I am giddy.

I also feel slightly nauseated. Not from car sickness, but rather from the idea that I've lost my mind and I can hear imaginary conversations around all the kitchen tables.

Did you know that Myra Katherine is leaving town to write a book? Why? Who's going to read her book? What is she thinking? Who does she think she is, anyway?

PEARL

A woman in my mid-forties, I am running away from home. With the full support of my family, I might add. They've grown weary of hearing me talk about the book I'm going to write someday. "Someday" has apparently arrived. Their gift to me is a week of solitude to get 'er done. Well, to get 'er started, at least. An avid collector of pithy, inspirational sayings, I immediately think of Mary Poppins.

"Well begun is half done," I quote aloud. My whole life has felt well begun. But sadly, half done. I start talk-texting in the "notes" feature on my phone. Seriously; I'm cool like that.

Once I arrive at my destination, the hostess unlocks the door to my (humble is the only fitting word) suite, swings it open, and tosses the key onto the nightstand, informing me that I won't need it because nobody locks their doors around here, and then reminds me of the gourmet meal that awaits in a few hours, and reminds me not to be late.

Someone is cooking for me? Not a chance in Hell I'll be late for that. Food is my love language. Food that someone else cooks for me is my love-love language.

"I'll be there," I say, giving her my confident, wish-that-I-could-afford-braces smile that reminds folks of Reese Witherspoon's, and watch the door close behind her. I set my suitcases and briefcase on the floor.

That was a joke. I don't own a briefcase.

I kick off my shoes, immediately put them back on (Did I mention the humble suite?) and sink onto the bed, which makes a weird crackling sound. I lift the corner of the bedspread, top sheet, and fitted sheet. Just as I suspected, the mattress is swathed in a protective plastic sheath. Ugh. I probably don't want to know why.

Well, I'm not here to nap; I'm here to write. An incredible feeling of freedom sweeps over me. As an owner of a personal-training studio in Fremont, Nebraska, I relish the prospect of a whole week with no classes, no sessions, and no appointments. As a mother — and stepmother and step-grandmother of too many to count — I can only imagine all that I will accomplish in a week with no carpool, no backpacks, and no school lunches. Only time.

And quiet . . .

Ok, whatever. It's not too many to count. It's eight. Eight is the actual number of children and grown children in my blended family. I'll only be writing about the two I actually grew in my body. And pushed out of said body without an epidural. Consider it payback.

Quiet . . .

PEARL

It's too quiet. And now all I can think about is that I want another baby.

I carry my bags into the writing room, and breathe. Full, deep breaths. As opposed to the short, choppy ones I usually take, followed by whiffs on my inhaler.

Three walls of this room are all windows, and the view is as grand as the suite is humble. I dig through bag after bag after bag and finally find my computer. I will never tell anyone that for a few brief minutes I feared that I had left it in Nebraska. I can hardly tear my eyes away from the view to focus on which wire goes where. Outside, autumn leaves drift on their circular paths to the ground, their colors so vivid I can almost hear how they will crunch when I walk on them later.

I plug in my computer, then reach back into my bag for a note that my daughter gave me earlier this morning. I pin it to a bulletin board covered with information about local hot spots and restaurants.

But first, a shower. To wash away the travel funk and clear away the cobwebs. A clean body and a clear mind. I poke my head into the bathroom and behold a toilet, sink, and bathtub. Where's the shower?

DAY ONE

It occurs to me that I cannot write a book in a place without a shower. This was a dumb idea. Time to go home.

No. I can do this. I can do hard things. I can wash my hair in a bathtub.

Like any good Southern girl, I evoke the mantra of Scarlett O'Hara in Margaret Mitchell's *Gone With the Wind*. "I won't think about that right now. I'll think about that tomorrow."

I say this out loud. Preaching to myself is so much more helpful than listening to myself. To break the blessed silence, to chase away the ghosts (and absurd thoughts of having another baby), and to finally ask myself how I feel about things. With no one to hear me answer.

I wash my face. Who needs clean hair, anyway? I return to the writing desk, open my laptop, and begin.

"Those who dive into the sea of affliction, bring up rare pearls."
~ Charles H. Spurgeon

PEARL

It would seem I've decided to write a book. It's not so much that I've decided it. It's that I've announced it. Like I've said it out loud, y'all. To people.

Bless my heart.

I've told my friends, my family, and my children. (Which, I get, is technically covered under family.)

I gave an extremely eloquent and impassioned speech about chasing dreams and following calls. And now I need medication. Whatever, in all of this beautiful world, gave me the idea that I could write a book?

I am scared.

Of not finishing. Of finishing. Of failing. Of succeeding.

I'm scared of disappointing my eight-year-old, who's already planning a book tour. To Mexico. Evidently, my book is going to be huge in Mexico. Hopefully, we can get there before the wall is built. And back in, again.

Sorry. There will be no politics in this book. Except when there is. In fact, I totally plan to solve the healthcare crisis.

Who knew healthcare could be so complicated? I knew. I'm smart like that. I'm not actually that smart. Everybody knew. Like that.

DAY ONE

So here's the thing. You are invited. Into my head; into my dancing thoughts. Since I was a child, words have swirled in my brain, and I'm forever searching for a new word, the right word. *Le mot juste*, the French call it. And when my head hits the pillow, the words dance.

(For the record I had to Google that. My dancing words are rarely in French.)

In the quiet, before sleep, I tell stories to my heart. And now you're invited on an adventure. I'll tell my story. You'll read your own.

We'll go on an adventure beyond the wall. Beyond the walls that you've built and I've built. And we'll go together. All the way to Mexico.

It's time to dive for pearls.

I stand up, stretch, touch my toes a few times and do a couple of jumping jacks to send oxygen to my brain. My back is on fire, and I'm reminded that sitting is the new smoking. Outside I watch through the window as a group of tourists attempt to tour the town on motorbikes. The Writers' Colony is atop a huge hill and I'm amused that people who probably can't even ride bikes have decided to try ones with motors. They are stuck and I'm both amused and annoyed. They are loud and disturbing on one hand and gloriously hysterical on the other. Plus, they haven't gotten the message that smoking is the old sitting.

Do they not understand that I'm working here?

Okay, back to the pearls. What, exactly, do I want to say? To whom? And why? Who do I think I am I to tell anyone anything about how to live their lives? And who do I think I am that anyone would want to read about mine?

I decide to write later. The glorious outdoors can wait no longer, and I need some fresh air. Arkansas air is the best air. Plus, maybe this scary *I'm an imposter and I know it* feeling will vanish by the time I return. I pull on my walking shoes, slip my room key (the one that I technically don't need), a little cash, and a credit card into the pocket of my jacket, smoosh my blonde bob into a messy-bun, and head out. I'll be gone twenty minutes, tops.

While I walk, I pray. And when I come back, two hours later, I write.

"I'm a pencil in the hand of God."

~ Mother Teresa

I've come to The Writers' Colony at Dairy Hollow — for one short week — to see if a book, written in the fire, can find its way from the ashes.

The colony is a fascinating place. Nestled in the northwest corner of the Ozark Mountains, in the historic arts village of Eureka Springs, I find everything about it rustic and quaint. Old buildings and cracked sidewalks. And by cracked, I mean that it looks like a three year-old was given cement to play with.

Homes here are built on cliffs. For real. There are stilts that rise from the bottoms of mountains that serve as foundations.

It's gorgeous. Trails loop in and out, and there are staircases in the middle of town that seem to lead to nowhere, or maybe to Heaven, and the houses are packed together with bed and breakfasts and hotels and bars. As I'm out walking, I pass a place called Twice Born. As in "born again."

PEARL

I go in. I buy my daughter, Emma Claire, a set of rubber bracelets that say "faith" and "courage" and all good words. I'm hoping that she'll wear them. Currently she likes to wear an assortment of ponytail holders on her wrist. Apparently, it's fashionable. Apparently, so is saying, "apparently."

And "fashionable."

I continue to walk, and notice a sign that reads, "Romantic Adventures." What the Hell, I think. Nobody knows me here.

I put my hand on the door and see another sign. This one reads, "You must be eighteen to enter this establishment."

So I walk away. Because, if seventeen is too young, than forty-four is

Way.

Too.

Old.

And then I go back. And I make a purchase. And then I hide the "you have to be eighteen" bag inside the "I've been born again" bag, so that even the strangers on the street won't know that my husband Mike and I do (ya know) romantic stuff.

DAY ONE

As I shove bag into bag, I look up to see an older gentleman, I'm guessing late sixties to early seventies, coming out of the Basin Park Hotel. He is wearing a pink night gown. And a pink robe. Apparently, this is normal here, as no-one but me seems to pay him any mind.

I continue to walk. I continue to pray. "God, I want to be a pencil in your hand. This is my earnest prayer. This is my holy hope."

One time, I accidentally stuck a pencil in my hand. (I hope "accidentally" was redundant and unnecessary). I pulled it out too fast, and passed out.

When life shows up as a pencil poke, we jerk it out. We are not a culture content to sit with the hurt. To sit with the hard.

But what if we did? What if we could? What if we could welcome, lean into, and even embrace the pencil in our hand? The pain in our hearts. What if, instead of watching from afar, waiting for others to get their shit together, we could walk beside our people and admit that our shit is pretty scattered, as well?

I tried to write this book year one after my divorce. Then again in year two, and year three. In much the same way that I jerked out the pencil. Fast. I passed out. And the dancing words passed on.

PEARL

So I decided to sit with the pencil — sit with my grief and wait.

Now I'm ready.

I have placed on the shelf my most beloved symptom. Maybe "symptom" is the wrong term. Maybe "side effect" is better.

Victimhood. The most lingering side effect from my divorce is playing the victim. Being the victim. Crying "victim."

I'm not ready to completely bury the idea of my being a victim. But I am ready to put it on the shelf. There's comfort in knowing it's there, like a book that I once read, and think someday I might want to read again.

Mrs. Charles E. Cowman wrote, "Great books are born in the furnace."

That's not to say that a book will be great simply because it was born in the furnace. But in order for it to have a chance at all of being great, a book must have been born in the fire. Tested in the fire. It must have survived the fire.

This book was born in the fire. The story of Pearl already exists. All I have to do is take the pencil out of my hand and place it in His.

This is fun. So I write some more.

> "Sometimes God redeems your story by surrounding
> you with people who need to hear your past,
> so it doesn't become their future."
> ~Jon Acuff

Okay. I hear you, Lord.

I get it. I need to be led by You as I write this week. But to whom are we writing? Who needs to hear this message that I have such a burning need to write?

Women, clearly. Scared women. Faithful women. Doubting women. Fighting-for-joy women. Neglected and abused women. Christian women. Childless women.

Mothers. Scared mothers. Faithful mothers. Sure-they-are-screwing-up-their-children mothers. Doubting mothers. Neglected, abused, Christian, mourning mothers.

Wives. Wives fighting to stay. Wives fighting to leave. Wives who know that life's too short. Wives who know that life's way too long.

My stomach rumbles. It's still hours before the European-style gourmet communal dinner that the Writers Colony is famous for, where I'll meet the other writers who are staying here. I'm both excited and terrified by the prospect.

I start digging through my bags. Empty of food. How did I eat my entire snack stash on the drive down? I'll have to stock up tomorrow. I need caffeine. I'm so sad that I gave up Diet Coke. Diet Coke was my friend, but I know if I can write a book without it, there's nothing that can ever stop me. Next? World Peace.

I settle for making a cup of tea. There are no chemicals and no bubbles, but it'll do. Now that I know who my audience is, fueled by caffeine and determination, I forge ahead.

"Snoring is the sweetest music in the world.

Ask any widow."

~ Elisabeth Elliot

My "married momma" friends come in all shapes, sizes, pedigrees, professions, educational levels, faiths, and so on, and yet I've figured out a very scientific way to boil us all down into only two groups.

Group A: This is my group. These are the women who have lain in bed next to their snoring husbands, and wondered how long they could hold a pillow over their beloved's mouth to effectively stop the snoring but not, you know, actually kill him.

Orange is not group A's color.

A's have pushed, nudged, and kicked; and for the love of all that is good and holy, they just want to get some sleep.

Group B: You fall into Group B if you think I'm a terrible, horrible person for acknowledging group A exists, and you are contemplating whether you should keep reading. Yes. Keep reading.

PEARL

Marriages. Also two types: A: The marriage you fight to keep, and B: the marriage you fight to leave. Don't be jealous; I've had both.

Fight for your marriage. Fight to save it, protect it, honor it, OR, fight to leave it.

Our backyard (which technically is our side yard, but for whatever reason feels like the backyard) has a patch of luscious, tall, green weeds. The girl who mows for us (please don't ask why we hire out our lawn service when we have two very capable boys) skipped this entire patch. Her dad later told me she thought they were flowers.
Weeds. Masquerading. It's annoying how easily we can be fooled.

And by "we," I mean me.

And it's possible I'm no longer talking about grass.

Anyway, in the midst of this hot mess of a side-back-yard, we actually have a beautiful hydrangea bush. In the fall, it bursts with huge puffs of color. I cut these and I dry these and I save them, and then at Christmas time I paint them.

(Seriously. If you know nothing else of this Southern girl turned Midwest momma, know this: There's nothing you can't spray-paint. I learned that at my mother's knee. One time my mom spray-painted acorns a beautiful shimmery gold for her Thanksgiving table, and while her guests were eating, tiny little bugs started marching out on the table. My mother, ever the gracious hostess, never said a word. She just quietly and discreetly smooshed the bugs and swept them under the table.)

Back to the side yard. One year, I noticed a tiny vine that was ever so innocently growing amidst the hydrangea bush. Beautifully green and subtle, I almost missed it. Last year, sadly, I did miss it. And that sweet little vine strangled the life out of my bush.

I was married for almost fifteen years and I, too, thought the patch of weeds were flowers. They were not. They were strangler vines.

Speaking of strangler vines, I could seriously strangle myself for not packing groceries. The closest Wal-Mart is thirty miles away. Why didn't I grab lunch when I was out buying faith bracelets and romance enhancers? Oh, wait. I did. Why is writing making me so hungry?

I dig in my purse and find a stick of gum and a ZONE bar.

Ha ha. Another joke. I don't carry a purse. My family thinks it's because if I don't have a purse, I'll never be asked to pay.

Cannot for all the world understand why they think that.

ZONE bar. Well, at one time it was. Now it's melted goo in a plastic wrapper. I unwrap one end, lick the extra from the wrapper (What? I'm alone!), and wash it down with another cup of tea that I wish was Diet Coke.

I glance at the clock. One hour until I can feed my love language with real food in the dining room. Until then, I have an empty screen to fill.

"Sometimes you'll never know the value of a moment until it becomes a memory."

~ Dr. Seuss

We were headed to Six Flags Over Texas. In July. Because what could be more fun than that?

We were one seatbelt, actually an entire seat, short and so we made the obvious choice. We gave the tallest person in my family the shortest straw. My mother, Cindy. Or CeCe, as she is affectionately called by her grandchildren.

CeCe rode for an hour, legs scrunched in length-wise down the middle aisle of my van.

She was wearing cute little travel pants. The kind that don't get wrinkled when you pack them. Or when you ride on the floor of a minivan.

When we finally arrived, she slowly tried to stand up, but noticed that she was a little bit stuck. Something on the floor was sticky, and now it was stuck on her pants. Goo. Slime. Putty. We'll never know for sure.

I played dumb. She had quite obviously gotten the slimy, sticky, goo-putty somewhere else because, if nothing else, I keep a clean car. Okay, I don't keep a clean car. And when you travel alone with two kids and two dogs as often as I do, it's not even a goal.

(I once heard a Superintendent of Schools speaking about class size. Reducing class size was not a district goal, simply for the fact that it unrealistic to think it could happen. My van is like a classroom with too many students and not enough teachers. And not enough seats.)

Keeping it clean is an unrealistic goal.

PEARL

We had three choices, none of them good: Leave Six Flags; search Six Flags until we found a pair of pants that my mother would be seen in publicly; or try to remove the putty stain from the seat of Mom's pants.

She waited in a restroom stall while my sister and I scrubbed, rubbed, and washed, and I still remember the sound of my sister's fingernails scraping away at the slime, which at this point was fairly recognizable as modeling clay, or Play-Doh.

Don't judge. How many cross-country trips have you taken alone with a two and five year-old? You need stuff. Sticky stuff. Fun stuff. (Arkansas is not really considered by most to be cross-country; it technically is. It's the vertical part of the cross.)

Anyway.

We finally removed the Play-Doh and then put Mom's pants under the hand dryer. Guess what, y'all? There was a flippin' hole. A hole! In CeCe's pants!

My sister and I looked at each other with horror. No woman who refuses to walk around Six Flags with a little goo on her pants is going to agree to walk around Six Flags with a hole in them.

We had two things going for us. First, my mother's vision is not great. She did not notice the hole. Secondly, my mother wears underwear. (Which I only mention because some people don't. I mean I think some people don't.)

Ok. Whatever. I don't.

We decided not to tell my mom. We decided to let her enjoy Six Flags. In July. In Texas. Blissfully unaware of the hole.

It was several months later, when she visited Nebraska wearing those same pants, that I realized I needed to come clean. Ha! Get it? Come clean?

Sorry; my son loves it when I do that. (He doesn't really love it.)

So. This is the story. My story. The story I share when asked to talk about divorce. What's it like? Well. It's like scraping goo out of pants. You're left with a hole.

The Bible says, in Matthew 19:6, "What God has joined together, let no man separate." I always considered that a command. I now consider it an imperative. What God has joined together, no man CAN separate.

And when you try (to fight for it) and when you do (fight to leave it) and when you file (for divorce) and when you sign (the papers) it feels a lot like my Mother's pants. You can't separate a marriage, separate a life, without creating a mess.

And leaving a hole.

It doesn't mean it's not the right thing to do. It might still be good and right and holy and life-saving and life-giving, but it's also a hard thing. The hardest thing.

I've often said that divorce is a death. Well, it's not just me. Smart-therapy people say it too. I knew two young women who became widows way too early, and y'all want to know something? I was jealous. They lost their husbands to death. I lost mine to divorce (or perhaps to something way before that) but he was gone, and I was widow.

Yes, jealous. When your husband dies, people bring you food. They send flowers. They love on you. And there's no judgment.

Can you imagine a widow hearing, "I'm so sorry about the death of your husband. But seriously, why did you take him to Methodist Hospital? Baptist is known for their cancer treatments." or "Y'all didn't go to Mayo Clinic? Idiots!"

DAY ONE

Nobody judges you when your spouse dies. I guess unless you actually were the one who killed him. With the pillow. For snoring.

So, here's the thing. Pretend we're sitting on my imaginary porch. (It has huge columns, a swing, and wispy ferns hanging from the ceiling. Tea is being served - Duh.) You ask for counsel regarding your marriage.

I will ask you, "Do you love him? Does he love you? Does he love Jesus? Is your marriage mostly amazing and partly he annoys the shit out of you? Then, my sister, you've gotta fight to stay."

I will also ask you, "Are you safe? Are you cared for? Can you breathe? Is your marriage an endless cycle of surviving neglect and adultery and abuse and then ignoring the neglect and adultery and abuse? Then fight to leave."

But if you leave, when you leave, remember the hole. Remember that separating what God joined together gets messy and it's hard and it's ugly and only Jesus can make it well. Only He can bring beauty from the ashes. Give thanks for Jesus.

And then give thanks that you're wearing underwear.

PEARL

And finally, when your friend gets divorced, love hard. Bring food and show mercy. Bring flowers and bring grace. And bring panties. Pretty ones. Good ones. None of that bunchy, scrunchy cotton stuff. Your friend is wearing the Big Red D now. It's more important than ever for her tush to be free of the dreaded pantyline.

I close my laptop and gaze out again on the picture-postcard view, now complete with a harvest moon that defines the word "October." It's time to go meet the writers. Hunger trumps shyness. I go.

Saturday, October 29, 2016

"Do it Afraid."

~ Sharon Irving, The Belong Tour

I awaken on my second day at the Writers' Colony drenched in sweat. Even as a write, I realize this is way too much information, but my peri-menopausal night sweats, combined with the crunchy mattress protector, made for a poor night's sleep. I look at the clock. It's 4:30 a.m. This totally bums me out for a millisecond because I'd hoped, with no obligations, to sleep in, but then I realize I'm not tired at all and this gives me more time to write.

I find all available forms of caffeine, make a bowl of oatmeal, and smile. It occurs to me that last night I ate with strangers. I ate with actual, real writers. Writers who are published and have editors and whose ACT scores were higher than the drinking age.

What?

Yes, I realized I ate with these women and I listened to these women and I didn't die. Go, me!

Scary Stuff

(I know I should think of a better word than stuff. It's a lazy word.) I'm scared of being lazy. I'm also scared of:

Not spending enough time with my children

Spending too much time with my children

My children

Crowds (By crowds, I mean more than three people)

People

(Donald Trump. Ex-wife-in-laws.)

The doorbell. When it rings, my children and I freeze

And we hold our breath until the threat

of imminent doom passes,

or until the UPS man leaves my package

The carpool lane

Fear. All action is communication, right? I learned this somewhere. And communication is either based in fear or based in love. (I learned that somewhere too. Either that or I made it up. I can't remember.)

Hiding behind the couch until the Schwan's man leaves would be an example of fear-based communication.

In the midst of the 2016 Presidential Election, I'd like to offer that love cannot trump hate. Until love trumps fear. Until empathy is our battle cry.

If we would give up the idea that speaking louder is speaking better, and if we would give up the idea that different is wrong, and if we would give up the idea that if you're not with us, you're against us, the world would split right open. And reveal the light.

In my little Nebraska town, there was recently a ginormous debate about a chicken plant. Chickens, y'all.

Bless our hearts.

I listened as the outsider that I am. "It'll smell," they said. It will smell? Seriously? We are an agricultural town in an agricultural state. There are feed lots surrounding us on all sides. We have a pork-processing plant. We have a dog-food production company. I don't mean to be ugly, but our town already smells.

PEARL

Many people had legitimate economic and environmental arguments about the chicken plant, but I can assure you that the "it'll smell bad" theory was not one of them. When the kids and I first arrived in this town I've grown to love almost six years ago, it was a beautifully warm day in February. I prepared a picnic because, for whatever reason, eating outside is fun.

We laid out our blanket and set out our food when Coulter, then five, looked up at me with a horrified expression.

"Mom! What is that smell?"

I burst into tears and cried, "Coulter! That's the smell of Fremont."

This. Another example of fear-based communication.

We aren't scared about smells. We aren't even scared of chickens. (Well, maybe a little bit about chickens.) We're scared because chickens will bring people. People who don't look like us or dress like us or worship like us.

We will travel thousands of miles across countries and oceans to spread the Gospel of Jesus. We want you to know about Him. But not here. Here's too close. You are too dark and too different and we don't want our town to smell.

DAY TWO

Of fear. And racism.

There's talk of building a wall. Protecting our borders. Berlin, anyone?

Where was I? Empathy.

What if? What if you could believe with your whole being that I am wrong, and yet still seek to understand me? What if I could absolutely and passionately disagree with you, and yet still seek to hear you? To know you. To learn from and about you.

I'm scared, y'all. I'm scared of too much and not enough and too soon and too late. Scared of fear in our hearts masquerading as hate. Scared to speak up and scared to be quiet.

You're scared of dark men wearing tunics. I get that. Can you get that I'm scared of angry white men in power? You're scared of terrorists. I'm scared of walls. We are all scared. Can we just be scared together?

Can we do the hard things, and do them scared? Do them afraid? Maybe one day love will trump fear, but until that day, what if we act anyway? What if we love, anyway?

— More Scary Stuff

My children will grow up and leave

My children will grow up and never leave

Four-way stops

Divorce

Not being known

Being known

Cats (sorry)

New math

Old math

Any kind of math

What if we're not fearless? And what if that's okay? We can parent and teach and learn and listen and we can love. And we can do it afraid.

— Even More Scary Stuff

People who put up Christmas lights
before Thanksgiving

Atheists

Atheists who put up Christmas lights
before Thanksgiving

Forgetting people's names

Forgetting my own name

Forgetting to be brave

Forgetting that I don't have to be brave

Forgetting that you don't have to be brave

Forgetting to love you because you are scared

Forgetting to love you because I am scared

Let's just get on with living this one glorious life, y'all. Yes?
And if we're scared? Then let's do it afraid.

PEARL

I make a grocery run. I need snacks. I stumble upon a quaint, organic-type healthy-eaters store. It reminds me of the dichotomy that is Eureka.

That is me.

I get the idea that if I use the front door, I'll find apples and berries and fancy cheese. But if I'm brave enough to venture toward the back door, I'm certain I'll find items with more of a hemp-type origin.

Did you know that you can buy marijuana gummy worms?

I don't need many groceries. The dinners here, besides being delicious, provide a day's worth of calories, in any case. And that's before dessert. When I tease about the calorie overload, the writers remind me that it's all healthy food. True, but my skinny jeans don't care if my calories are healthy. Truth is, if I keep eating like this, come Friday, they're not gonna fit.

And my fat jeans will also be iffy.

DAY TWO

I smile with relief as I trudge back with my purchases. (It's uphill both ways, somehow.) Fremont is perfectly flat and I'm out of hill shape.

But I'm happy. Nobody gave me the side-eye last night; just welcomed me into the fold and asked what I was working on. The fact that I had trouble describing my project, exactly, didn't faze them.

When they dug deeper I changed the subject to politics.

I showed them a picture of my younger brother, a top aide to Hillary Clinton, standing next to her on a plane. They are laughing. He's wearing a pink cowboy hat as a joke, and there is joy. I wonder why others can't see the Hillary that he knows. The Hillary that I see. I'm proud of my brother, and talking about what a big deal he is is much safer than talking about what a has-been I am.

They gasp at my pictures, ask question after question, and I am safe. I'm answering their questions while also listening to the demon voices of self-doubt.

What is it that I'm writing? Hell if I know. But here. Look at my brother. He's cool.

PEARL

"I fully believe that one of the greatest gifts I've given my children is the example of a mother who pursues her passions like a motherf@#%er."

~ Cheryl Strayed.

I know. I'm sorry. You bought this book thinking that a politically liberal, socially conservative Christian would never use such strong language.

Three things happened when I turned forty. Well, to be specific, more like forty-two. Or three. I'm trying to remember when I got re-married.

One, I started having lots of sex. See why the marriage-date and age is important?

Two, I discovered vodka. Most of my friends drink wine. I don't understand this. Most wine is bitter and laden with calories.

Vodka, on the other hand is clear. It's practically water. But when you engage in a texting argument with your ex-wife-in-law regarding what you can and cannot call your second husband's youngest son from his second marriage, well then a little sip of the clear stuff works even better than my inhaler.

DAY TWO

For the record that's what I'm supposed to call him: "Mike's youngest son from his second marriage." In some circles "stepson" would be good and appropriate. That is not my circle. I live in a triangle.

Backstory. I grew up in a dry county. I embraced the tee-totaling ways of my parents and never had a drop of alcohol until I turned forty. Except for that time when my cousin's Coke was actually a can of rum and Coke. And that time my mother and I were served sparkling wine (not the bitter stuff) made from peaches grown in the south of France at some froufrou Italian place owned by the Mario guy from the cooking channel, and here's the thing: we had to drink the wine because it was given to us "compliments of the chef." We'd also been given sardines "compliments of the chef" and my teetotaler mom forced me to eat them, so as not to embarrass our family. (We were there as friends of the President — not the current one — the Arkansas Clinton one.) So I can assure you that when the peachy-wine-goodness came out, I told her we had no choice.

"We must do it for the family," I said.

To summarize, rum and Coke at eight, peach wine at twenty-five, and now, at forty-four I'm a recovering teetotaler who drinks vodka. I think it makes me a nicer person.

PEARL

You thought I forgot the third thing, but I didn't.

I started using the f-word. Well, not really. I started reading and quoting other women who use it. These things take time. When I first read Anne Lamott's *Traveling Mercies*, I skipped over the bad words. Now when I read it, I say them out loud.

I get it now. Sometimes, only the f-word will do. Sometimes the polite word, the refined and educated word, is not the right word. I also understand that not everyone is comfortable with the f-word; that it can be harsh and offensive. If I ever hear my own children use it, I'll slap them across the head and send them to a monk-led boarding school.

Just kidding. I would never slap my children.

Emma Claire has recently started saying, "Jeez." For the record, I find this much more offensive than the f-word. It's short for Jesus, which is breaking the commandment about not taking the name of the Lord in vain. A friend suggested that Emma Claire say, "peanut butter and jelly," instead. Saying f@#% is not mentioned in the commandments, but out of respect for my readers, I'll just stick to f@#% for purposes of this book.

Which, technically, is still an f-word. Pardon my French.

Okay, so I can probably Google this, but why do people say, "Pardon my French?" That's so weird. "I am so tired of these damn politicians! Pardon my French." Seriously? Is "damn" even a French word?

One time, having been placed at a table with strangers who quickly became friends, this woman was sharing her childbirth stories and said, "So this nurse comes in and she says 'your baby might die,' and I'm like, 'What the f@#%?' Who says that to a new mother?"

And then she turns, just to me, and says, "Pardon my French." And then we die laughing because, again, is "f@#%" a French word?

It's also funny that she instinctively knew to pardon herself. Only to me.

(Ironically, the exact same thing happened to me when my son Coulter was born. He was just hours old when the doctor came in and said, "Your son could die." Same circumstances. Same possible virus. Only I didn't say, "What the f@#%?" (because I was only thirty-two and I didn't use that perfectly apt word back then).

Passions. I think that's where my dancing words started. Yes, somehow I started out wanting to discuss pursuing our passions, but it turned into a discussion of learning to say the f-word.

PEARL

How do you balance your passions? How are you perfectly present with your children and family while pursuing your dreams like a — well, you know.

We practice. That's how we do it.

Every day we practice the balance of being present as a mother and being present as a lover because in the everyday moments that string together a life, your children must see you pursuing and planning and dreaming and being. They must see your passionate heart.

It's okay for them to know they are your most important work but they are not your only work and they are your most perfect gift but they are not your only gift and it's okay for them to see the "dreams hidden beneath the coils of your bones." Really. It's okay.

Really okay. For them to know that motherhood is not your only dream. Not your only love. Not your only passion.

I was terrified to tell my eight-year-old daughter, Emma Claire, that I was leaving town for a week to pursue my passion. I didn't think she'd understand. I thought there would be tears and drama and lots of clinging. In truth, I greatly overestimated myself and underestimated my daughter.

First she squealed with delight and asked if she could spend the week at her friend Elena's house. Next, she wrote me a note that read, "I'm going to miss you for dear life, but Wow! Mom! You're going to be an author!" And finally, she planned our book tour to Mexico.

She got it right.

If nothing else happens this week, if there is no book and there are no readers and there is no book tour to Mexico, it is still very "well with my soul."

This week away just might be the best parenting decision I've ever made. I didn't put them first. I put them best, and in so doing, taught my children to chase their dreams like a mother.

Ack. Writing about my kids brings a wave of homesickness I haven't anticipated. I'm missing my littles who aren't really so little anymore and I reach for the phone.

They're at school.

PEARL

There's a park just outside my window, and I can hear preschoolers squealing. My first thought is one of annoyance, much like I feel about the motor-bikers (motorcyclist-wannabe's) that screech up my hill, but then I decide squealing children is exactly what I need.

I unplug my laptop and head down the path. There are no tables, but I find a shade tree to sit beneath while I listen and write.

Sometimes a mother needs to hear the sounds of children, even if not her own.

I have to try to hold my emotions in check this week. I don't have the luxury of feeling sorry for myself, of getting lost in my journals, getting lost in my head. There is a discipline that keeps me going. But here on the dirt, I lose it.

Soren Kierkegaard wrote that "the most painful state of being is remembering the future." There under the trees, I allow myself to remember the future that I won't have.

A man walking his dog looks at me. His eyes reveal sadness and empathy and he smiles knowingly and continues on.

I hear children laughing again. It's a welcome interruption. I gather my things and walk back to my room.

"You ever notice how 'What the Hell?' is always the right answer?"

~ Marilyn Monroe

I promised you pearls. Consider this your first one. If someone comes to you and tells you they are leaving their husband, "What the Hell?" is always appropriate and right. If you're a Southern girl like me, you might feel it's improper to use such language. If that's the case, a simple, "Bless your heart" will do. For the record, they mean the same thing.

I heard it all. "God hates divorce," was my favorite.

It was not my favorite.

My friend Jean nailed it. No mention of the fire and damnation that awaited me and my children, she said simply, "What the Hell?"

Southerners are, at all times, appropriate. While the rest of the country thinks wearing white only between Memorial Day and Labor Day is a silly and outdated rule, I can assure you that Southerners do not. I wore white tennis shoes in April once and I'm still feeling regret.

PEARL

Southern women wear pearls. We own sterling. Even if all we can afford is a bowl of ramen, we will bless that food and eat it with the finest of silver and we know (like I'm sharing with you now) that if someone blesses your heart, behind that perfect smile, they are really saying, "What. The. Hell?"

Or they might be saying, "F@#% you."

It's hard to tell, and it could go either way.

But if a Southern woman says, "Bless your heart; what the Hell?" and then brings you a casserole, just know that your life is pretty much over.

The park was a good idea.

The children, too — a good idea.

Together with the public display of emotion (the ugly-cry!) they've given me the courage to open my journals and revisit the hardest of all days.

"Whatever this moment holds, accept it as if you chose it."

~ Eckhart Tolle

I woke up early on the final day. The final day. The really final day of my first marriage.

I wanted, so very much, to return to sleep, but my mind kept racing back to the past December, to a day when my friend told me that her husband had been ill, but, "The doctors know it isn't cancer."

Less than a week later, it was cancer.

Less than a year after that, she was a widow.

And while I was headed to the courthouse to bury my marriage, she was headed to the cemetery to bury her husband. Cancer made her a widow. Divorce, for me, did the same.

But I was ready. And whatever this moment held, I was prepared to accept it as if I chose it. I'm ashamed to admit I didn't trust him to do what was right for our children. But I did trust Him.

PEARL

It was August. Coulter was starting third grade. He had no idea that across town decisions were being made and tears were being shed and papers were being signed. He just knew that his new teacher was Mr. Hamilton. And that Mr. Hamilton gives out candy for no reason at all.

Emma Claire went to daycare. She was nervous about saying the wrong things because she hadn't been there all summer. "Mom? Do you know that Mona doesn't like the word 'mousetrap?'"

No. Actually I did not know that.

My kids were oblivious. As they should be.

Parents should never bring their children into a drama that grown-ups can barely survive. Trusting your children with too much information and using them as "stand-in" spouses is child abuse. People who do that should go to jail. Young children should not know about your day in court.

I arrived at the courthouse. With my mom.

My attorney agreed that she could come so long as she didn't say anything.

We walked up the steps, put our purses through security, and I thought about the past few months and how, day after day, (after reading Mark Batterson's book, *The Circle Maker*) I had walked around the courthouse, praying and circling and singing, and I remembered this lady who used to walk around town with a parrot on her shoulder and we called her the crazy parrot lady, and I feel terrible now, because maybe she was just praying, and I have this feeling people think I'm the crazy parrot lady, just sans parrot, and there are probably some office ladies at the courthouse who gather around the window like the "Friends" characters used to do when Ugly Naked Man was in the apartment across the street, and they're all like, "Time for a smoke break. Crazy-praying-circling-singing-walking lady is back."

What happened next was nothing I could've ever prepared for.

First, there was no trial. I've gotta say; I really wanted a trial. I like to talk. I like microphones. I like talking into microphones.

I also like telling my story. Several months prior, during a pre-trial hearing, the judge had listened to the lies of my ex-husband's attorney. He looked at me and said, "Young lady, that is no way to live your life."

Yelling, "That's not how I'm living my life!" was not allowed, and I thought this hearing was finally my chance.

PEARL

But it wasn't.

My attorney went back and forth between the judge and Amazon lawyer lady, as my mom sat, painfully quiet, in the corner. Surprisingly, separating a life takes a lot longer than taking goo out of my mother's pants.

Emotional and weary, we waited. My attorney came in and said, "You are not f@#%ing going to believe this. He wants the f@#%ing silver. I have never known a f@#%ing man to want the f@#%ing silver."

I died laughing. You must remember two things. First, Southern women have sterling patterns. Patterns are passed down from generation to generation. We may not know where our next meal is coming from, but I can assure you, it won't come from selling the silver. Second, my mother didn't learn the f-word at the ripe, young age of 40. She learned it that day. Age 67. But I think even she would agree that, in that moment, it was the right word.

The only word.

I don't think my ex-husband really wanted the silver or thought for a fleeting moment that I'd give it to him. He was just mad.

I was madder. I kept my silver.

This was two years after Allen filed for divorce. I thought I would feel relief. I thought I would breathe easier. But instead, I had the breath knocked straight out of me. By a brick.

The judge said, and I quote, "Yada, yada, yada, irrevocably broken, blah blah."

He used that term, "irrevocably broken," over and over and over again. It was hard and freeing and healing and I just wanted to close my ears and shut him out. I wanted to cry, "No we're not!"

Because of Jesus, no one is. Not even us. The most broken of the broken.

The incredible thing about divorce, about the hearing, about the judge is this: You walk into that place of judgment to separate. And you leave that place with no other choice than to be united.

You leave broken and yet whole. You leave knowing that together you will love and nurture and protect and you know that you will do it well.

I turned to my attorney. I seriously loved this man. I was a pain in his ass from the day he met me, and I kind of loved that, too. He knew more about my life than any other person. More than my mom. More than my ex-husband.

PEARL

More.

He reached out his hand, as if to shake mine. I said, "Oh good grief. You know I'm going to hug you."

He replied, "Um, I'm not really comfortable with that." I hugged him. And then I walked to the other side of the room and I hugged the father of my children.

God used the two years of waiting; the two years between the no-longer and the not-yet to change me. To change my heart. To show me: You can do this.

I can do hard things. And I can do the hard thing after that.

St. Francis said, "First you do what's necessary, then you can do what's possible." I had done what was necessary.

And although I struggled to accept that moment as if I had chosen it, I had, in fact done that very thing. I had chosen this. And choosing was necessary.

I left the courthouse and went to see my Pastor. He pulled out a bottle of liquor. Something brown. Poured it over a small glass of ice. I cried. He listened. He affirmed.

I had done the necessary. Now, on to the possible.

DAY TWO

I vividly remember the Pastor's Kentucky Bourbon and its sweet amber glow that flowed over my tongue and filled my throat and spread through my chest until I began to choke and cough.

When Pastor first sat down, he offered me an empty glass with ice and a bottle of water. I poured the water over the ice and he laughed.

I didn't know about the stash of good stuff.

I hadn't yet given up the manna that is Diet Coke, so he offered to dumb-down my drink. Which, looking back probably made this adopted Kentuckian die just a little.

Why is it that I can remember drinking with my Pastor and yet I can't remember what to write about next?

I open up my journal that I've kept for twenty years or more.

PEARL

"If you aren't in the arena,
also getting your ass kicked,
I'm not interested in your feedback."
~ Brene Brown

One night, covers drawn and prayers lifted, Emma Claire said, "Mom? What kind of book are you writing? Is it a children's book?"

"No, dear. Not a children's book. I'm writing non-fiction."

"You should, totally write a tip book. Like, yes. Okay. Here it is. A tip book. Like Ten Tips for Parents! On how to be good parents!"

"Emma Claire, that's so sweet. You think I'm such a good mom that I should write a parenting book?"

She ponders that. Like maybe she had spoken too quickly. "Well, or, okay, how about maybe a tip book on beautiful rooms? Like, how to decorate."

Right now, the most beautiful room in our home has a full-size ping-pong table smack dab in the middle, because I can't figure out what to do with it. So let's do the parenting one.

When I finally did the hard thing and jumped into the divorce arena, my husband I were required, by Nebraska law, to attend a parenting class. I thought this was the dumbest thing ever. People have babies all the time who don't have a clue about children, and no such class is required. And yet, if you screw up your marriage, the government is confident you're gonna screw up your children, too, so you have to go to class.

Mine was taught by a woman who had never been married. Or had children. She wasn't in the arena.

The first thing she handed out was a Divorce Bill of Rights. And I remember reading it, thinking, Was this computer-generated? By a robot? A robot without children, without a spouse?

One of the mandates was that children should always come first. I disagree.

I had school lunch with Emma Claire the other day. (Well I didn't actually eat there, because on the menu was French toast sticks and green peas.) French toast sticks and green peas? What the Hell?

Bless all our dang hearts!

PEARL

Sitting across the table from us was a little guy who couldn't so much as get one of those smooshed up peas into his mouth without getting into trouble, and he was wearing a shirt that read: "I am the future." Lord, have mercy!

Looking at him reminded me of what happens when we put children first.

A few months into our separation, I found myself saying that a lot. "My children come first." The problem with it is that, as they grow and you have more than one child, who comes first? I found myself fighting battles (alone) and I couldn't figure out why nothing was ever enough.

More wasn't enough. More than that. Better than that. What I want. When I want it. Never enough.

Y'all.

Pearls number two and three: Children should not come first. Children should come best.

Months into my separation, I was reading statistics on children of divorce. It's not good. The dancing words landed on "best." What is best for my children?

What is best for Coulter? Here. Today. What is best for Emma Claire? And sometimes what's best for our children is to occasionally come second.

From my journal:

August 24th, 2009
Move God, or move me. I feel trapped and anxious.

August 27th, 2009
"I shall never think of anything that He has forgotten, so why I am I worried?" ~ Oswald Chambers. (But I am worried. And scared.)

August 28th, 2009
I'm starting to lose my confidence. God, give me boldness and not timidity. Give me the courage and grace to be authentic and true to my emotions and desires. Give me the wisdom I need so that the choices I make will be BEST for my children. I claim your promises for my life and for the lives of Coulter and Emma Claire. (In the margins, I add my ex-husband's name. I love how the word BEST was there the whole time.)

September 12, 2009

(More Chambers.) *"Beware of not acting upon what you see in your moments on the mount with God."* (But I didn't act.)

January 4, 2010

Happy New Year! I've decided to focus on re-claiming my effervescence. (My sister had previously mentioned that I had lost it.) *I'm going to be a better wife. A better mother. A more faithful servant of God. It's time to be happy.* (I don't know at what point I started believing the key to my marriage was for me to just be better. Do better. Try harder. Run faster.)

February 1, 2010

I heard about a book called, 'The Love Dare.' I'm starting today.

March 12, 2010

My husband doesn't want to have sex. Ever. I think this is weird, but I'm not sure. I can't believe I'm even writing this down. I wish I'd had sex in college. Lots of it. I wish that I knew what all the fuss is about. I wish I understood why my friends complain about having to have sex all the time. I wish I knew what it means to "make love." But this is just part of the "for better or worse." And I can do better. (I've gotten off track. Even in my journal. Starting to feel sorry for myself, when I know that I am the problem. And so I continue.) Change my heart, O God and renew a right Spirit within me. I will lose weight. I will buy candles. I will do better.

May 19th, 2010

Surprisingly, the Love Dare didn't work. So thankful to be in Arkansas (home). I don't know what's wrong with me. This week, my husband said he will never leave, because of the children. That is my greatest fear. That he'll stay. Only for them.

May 24th, 2010

My husband has a subtle way of talking down to me. I feel small. I'm so tired of feeling small. God move. Or move me.

May 27th, 2010
Tell the truth. Tell the truth. Tell the truth. I don't think my husband loves me. I no longer trust him. God, show me a way out. Give me a way out. A way that allows me to love and parent and raise my children. A way out that will honor you. Something, God. Anything.

June 8th, 2010
I'm too tired to write.
And the journal goes blank. That's it.

I wish I could tell you that God finally moved. Turns out, God doesn't move. And he doesn't move us. He doesn't kick us into the arena. We have to move ourselves.

Parenting tips (pearls) number four through nine:

Figure out what is best for your children, and do that.

Yes, I know. That was number two and number three. But that's it. That's the answer to every parental question. And for me, that's when the courage came. The moment I decided to tell the truth, not in spite of my children, but because of my children.

So. Here it is:

Pearl number ten: Don't you dare stay in a broken marriage "for the children."

Fight to stay, or fight to leave, but children do not deserve the burden of narcissistic, martyrdom-thinking. Just as it is never a child's fault when their parents divorce, it should NEVER be their fault that they didn't.

So. Holding my babies tight, I dove. And yes, my ass got kicked. Kicked real good.

PEARL

Day Three

Sunday, October 30, 2016

I wake up this morning feeling out-of-sorts. It's Sunday, and while I'm staying true to my "no outside media" policy, it seems, from what fellow writers are saying, that Donald Trump is gaining steam. How is it possible for a man who called a woman "too ugly to rape" to have the Christian vote?

Seriously. I need to be in church. But if I go to church, all the strangers will welcome me and be nice to me and they'll wonder why I'm here and, Heaven forbid, some sweet old lady who loves Jesus will ask me to lunch.

Really. I should really go to church. There are Hillary signs here. I think I even saw a Hillary sign on the Presbyterian Church lawn. Christians here probably understand that being pro-life means being "for life." For everyone's life. For all of their life.

PEARL

I'm pro-life, but by the way, I'm building a wall, so what I really mean is that I'm pro-American lives.

What the Hell is happening to me? I am not writing about politics, so why is it in my head?

Stop it. Dancing political words, stop!

I text my dad. He recently had a major medical trauma and in his free time of recovery (well not so much free time as work his ass off to get strong again time) he discovered Bitmoji. It's like a cartoon picture of my dad with texts that say things like, "You go, girl." They make me laugh, and my Dad thinks I can do anything, so when I'm feeling unsure, I send him a text.

So I text him now. Are we worried? Is Gregory worried? Should my writer friends who are now living vicariously through my brother be worried?

He texts back a Bitmoji that says, "It's all good."

I decided to skip church. I go for a walk instead. I can be with God anywhere.

> "Listen. Are you breathing just a little
>
> and calling it a life?"
>
> ~ Mary Oliver

I was sitting in an ob/gyn waiting room. We had just moved back to Nebraska — a new beginning for my then-husband Allen, me, and our children, ages six and two. I had felt a lump in my breast.

I waited, irritated by all the cute pregnant mommas, knowing that my baby-making days had passed.

The nurse came out. Guess what? She was twelve years old! What is it with these people? Does no-one have to go to college anymore? Except she was pregnant and maybe more like twenty-five.

Whatever. She was too young. She asked me if I had any special concerns. I came undone.

Un. Done.

She clicked her pen and told me the doctor would be right in.

PEARL

My doctor? Thirteen, maybe fourteen. "My nurse mentioned you might be upset."

I wanted to tell her that I was fine. It was just the move and the lump and the ridiculously beautiful baby bumps. I'm a liberal Methodist, conservative Christian and if you don't know anything about liberal Methodists, conservative Christians, well let me tell you, we are

Always.

Just.

Fine.

Thank you very much for asking.

But I couldn't tell her that. Instead something horrible came out of my mouth. "I think I hate my husband."

This word is horrible. I don't hate him. I love him. But I am so sad. Lost. I love him and I can't stand him. I can't stand what he's done to our family. And I can't stand this town, and I can't stand this life, and I can't find a job, and I just can't even. Ya know. Do this life thing.

She suggested that I might be depressed.

I laughed. Politically liberal, socially conservative Christians don't get depressed. It's called faith. Duh.

She continued, "I'm going to write you a prescription and I want you to come back in a month."

Is this woman serious? Doesn't she know that I'm one of the happiest, bubbliest people you'll ever meet? Except, well, when I'm not?

Back in my car, I stare at the prescription. I'm afraid that if I decide to dive (ever notice how divorce and dive are practically the same word?) my husband will use it against me.

I decide not to fill it.

But then.

This unemployed mom, living in a new town that smells like dog food, who may or may not hate her husband, who for sure doesn't hate her husband, so maybe it's herself that she hates, is driving around town with her two year-old, dropping off resumes.

This is an occasion that might call for a babysitter, but let's review. I had no job, and thus could not pay a babysitter. After the final stop and yet another rejection before I even had a chance to set said resume into their hands, I sat behind the steering wheel and wept. Silently. Only not silently, because Emma Claire heard me.

"Mom? Why are you always crying?"

Always.

Out of the mouth of babes. I drove straight to the pharmacy and filled my prescription. The pamphlet said that it would take ten to fourteen days for the medicine to take noticeable effect.

On the tenth day, I woke up and I knew. The fourteen year-old doctor had saved my life.

I was done with loving my husband and hating myself. I was done with caring about appearances. I was done with breathing just a little.

And calling it a life.

I want to take a break and maybe a walk, but then I think about all the people who think I'll fail or hope I'll fail; and I think of all the people who think I'll actually write this book and hope I'll actually write this book; and so for them—all of them, I skip the walk.

Instead I jog around the tiny apartment to wake up my brain and stretch my back. I then send a naked picture of myself to my husband, because it will shock him and make him laugh and remind him that he saved the best for last.

And then I worry that somehow our iClouds are connected, and what if my children get the naked picture, and I'm pretty sure that would scar them far worse than divorce, so I quickly delete the picture.

And with my ever-flattening bootie, I sit back in my chair and write.

> "Life is good. Be happy now. Let it go."
>
> ~ Pastor Otis

A friend recently mentioned how she wasted away her forty-ninth year by being "almost" fifty. She looked at me. Really looked and said, "When you're forty-nine, be forty-nine. Don't waste it. Don't miss it. Don't be almost fifty for an entire year."

PEARL

Don't almost be.

Surely that would be the most perfect way. Surely being here, being present, being now is how God arranged our time and ordered our days so, it really should be the most natural of ways to live —

Here.

Instead, we find ourselves longing for the past or trying to forget the past. Either way, too much time is spent there.

Other days are spent looking ahead. Too far ahead.

What if Coulter's only ambition in life is to master bottle flipping? God forgive us for the year bottle flipping became a talent. What if Emma Claire really moves to Paris to open a French bakery? What if I don't have enough money to retire, and what if I have to work forever and all my friends will be living in their retirement beach homes, and what if I'll be an eighty year-old Mimi stuck in the Midwest, shoveling snow and hoping somebody invites me to visit?

We're almost okay. We're almost there. Then we blink, and we're almost fifty. I'm almost happy. I'm almost finished, and it'll just be one minute more and one minute after that and I'm almost ready to pay attention to you, but not quite yet.

DAY THREE

The stars can't number how many times I have said to my children, "I'm almost ready."

Please play with us.

I'm almost ready.

Please read with us.

I'm almost ready.

Please jump with us.

I'm almost fifty.

I wonder if the "almost epidemic" is one of those beloved symptoms that Eugenia Price wrote about in *Share My Pleasant Stones*. I wonder if the race for more and better has left us victim to this idea that tomorrow will be better.

What if our lives are good and right and beautiful but in our frenzy of 'almosts', we miss it?

Brother Otis, a pastor from Lincoln, Nebraska used to close his sermons with this: "Life is good. Be happy now. Let it go."

Just weeks into his retirement, Pastor Otis was shoveling snow, had a heart attack, and died. See? I told you!

PEARL

Shoveling snow in retirement is no good. Please tell your friends to buy my book. And then please invite me to your retirement home. On the beach.

Life is good, y'all. Even when it's hard. And so often, because it is hard.

God calls us to live abundant lives, not almost lives. Be happy now. Not tomorrow. Not almost happy. And not a superficial happy, like when your stylist absolutely nails your hair color. Well, maybe be a little bit happy about that. Those of us born blonde, turned dirty blonde (what a horrific term, by the way) and then after baby after baby after baby started to look like Reese Witherspoon in that horrible movie where she goes brown, understand this. (And I can't even remember the movie, because all I remember is her brown hair.)

I tried going natural, not once but twice, and then I got a Word from the Lord. "Let your pasty white skin be a reminder never to go dark again." What? You didn't know Jesus cared about your hair color? Well, He does.

After the gothic brunette incident, I swung the other way. Way past center. I became a bleach blonde. Like all over blonde-goodness.

Bless my heart.

My friend and stylist at the time had, at one time, been besties with my husband's ex-wife. My second husband. His second ex-wife. I'm the third one. Let's keep up.

Evidently the bleach blonde thing was not working, and my mother gently suggested to me that I was the victim of a massive and cruel "let's cause her hair to fall out from too much bleach" conspiracy, spearheaded by the friend and the ex. Again, his ex. Not mine.

I told my mother she was being ridiculous, but then I remembered she'd been right about pretty much everything else for my entire life up to that moment, so she was probably right about the hair.

The Bible verse, "Be still and know that I am God" was originally translated from Hebrew as "Let it go." I'm not suggesting letting go if you are the victim of a vicious hair conspiracy, but rather letting go of tomorrow. Letting go of yesterday.

I wrestled with this translation for a time, because I strongly prefer the version where I'm just still. Where no action is required on my part. But to let something go is a verb. We have to open our tight fist and, with a breath light enough to wish on a dandelion, we have to send it out. And let it go.

PEARL

When we are almost something, we are not anything at all. If we are almost ready, we are not ready. If we are almost sure, we are not sure. If we are almost okay, we are not even close to being okay. And if we are almost fifty, we are still forty-nine.

I moved to the Midwest when I was twenty-two. Throughout my twenties and thirties, I lived in Nebraska, Minnesota, and South Dakota. But I never bought a winter coat.

I'm stubborn that way.

I had coats. Down south, these coats would probably pass for a winter coat. But winter coats—true cold-weather, keep-your-ass-from-freezing coats — are wack-a-do expensive. Every winter would come, and I would pause. We'll be moving south soon, I'd think. It's almost time.

Pretty much from the day I left Arkansas, I wanted to move home. Perhaps not buying a winter coat was an act of defiance. Spring would come and the wack-a-do expensive coats would go on sale and I'd consider it again. And pause. And so it went. For twenty years.

How does one not speak up about being cold? Eventually I learned to speak up.

DAY THREE

On our second date, I told the man who would soon become my second husband that I liked big diamonds and would be keeping my maiden name.

It had taken four hours at the social security office to officially change my name back to Hale, and I thought I would pass right out from being around all those people. I can't do it again.

Plus I've become a wild would-be feminist who uses the f-word and we're supposed to keep our names. It's a rule. And by wild feminist, I mean on paper. In my head. I can't actually do marches or protests or anything that might require me to leave my couch. Because of this character trait, I won't be burning my bras or organizing parades.

As a feminist, I know I'm beautiful without big diamonds. And makeup. And hair bleach.

But I'm my most beautiful feminist self when adorned with said diamonds, lots of mascara, and highlights. Ya know, while sitting on my couch. Writing about my strong feminist views.

Anyway. Coats.

It was December in New York City, and I was with my mother and sisters, and I saw it. At Saks Fifth Avenue. It cost seven hundred and eighty dollars, and was by far the least expensive coat on the floor.

My mom looked at me as if to say, "Are you sure?" Not necessarily because of the price (although that had to be part of it because in my adult life, she'd never known me to have the freedom to spend seventy dollars, much less seven hundred). And I was. I was sure.

Maybe we'd move south someday, and if so, I'd happily donate said coat to one of my less fortunate friends. And by less fortunate, I don't necessarily mean financially. I mean having to stay. In the cold.

All I knew was that I was tired of almost leaving—almost moving—almost going home for my entire life, and so I let it go.

I opened up my fist. Seven hundred eighty dollars and one dandelion-puff later, I let go of one of my most beloved symptoms. I let go of "almost."

Life is good, y'all. And even when it's not, let it go. Be happy now.

DAY THREE

A ZONE bar and about fifty thousand chocolate covered almonds for lunch. What is it about touristy towns that make you feel obligated to buy specialty nuts?

This cannot be good for my digestion. Or my skinny jeans.

And all this sitting. Lord-a-mercy with the sitting. Note to self, when I make it big (and by big I mean someone other than my parents and husband read my books), I'm investing in a standing table.

> "You own everything that has ever happened to you. Tell your stories. If people wanted you to write warmly about them, they should've behaved better."
>
> ~ Anne Lamott

An ultra-conservative, white, male, Baptist University professor recommended that I read Anne Lamott's *Traveling Mercies* when I was in my late twenties, which, if you've read the book, you'll see as ironic.

Maybe. Or maybe it was just weird. The recommendation, not the book.

I learned the faith of my parents as a member of the First United Methodist Church in a small town in Southwest

Arkansas. As you know, Methodists are quite liberal and forward thinking. Sorta. Not really.

I mean, how liberal can you be in a small town that not only refrains from selling alcohol to minors (you know, because of the whole "it's illegal" thing) but also from selling alcohol to adults because again, it's illegal. Still is. You think I'm kidding. I'm not.

Look it up.

But we thought we were liberal and that really was the point. It was only after reading Lamott's book that I realized how not-liberal I was. The experiences I had not had. The words I had not said. The grace and the mercy and the understanding that I had not offered, had not given, and had not received.

I listened to *Traveling Mercies* on a solo road trip.

Ohmygosh! I looked around to see if anyone else had heard what I heard. (I suppose outside my car, since there was no-one else inside my car.) She just said the f-word!

Lord, have mercy! She said it again. Can we say that? I mean, if we love Jesus, can we still say the f-word? I'm just asking. For you. The not-liberal. Because, whatever.

I use that word all the time. Seriously. I was raised by extremely politically liberal, loving, forward-thinking parents, who adhered to a strict socially conservative, Christian lifestyle, and expected the same from their children. Keep up. It's not hard.

Being liberal in the Bible belt meant that you cared for the least of these; you took your hand-me-downs to Irene; and you voted for Bill Clinton. I still have my Bill Clinton for Governor tee-shirt. I'm that liberal.

And it never occurred to us that it might be considered racist to take our hand-me-downs to Irene. Many years later it was suggested to me that it was. I'm not sure. Irene is like the Godfather of our black community. She would see to it that our clothes made it to the right family. (Technically she's more like the Godmother, but for some reason, Godfather sounds cooler.)

She is a large, kind, soft-spoken black woman who inherited the position from Mrs. Bell, also a large, kind, soft-spoken black woman.

As a side note, Mrs. Bell helped my mother. No. Not like "The Help."

Well. A little like "The Help."

PEARL

Life during the 1950's in Mississippi was nothing like life in Arkansas in the 1980's. We shared meals. We shared bathrooms. We shared life.

I never considered that this was in any way racist, and for the record, I still don't.

Mrs. Bell loved our family, and if she were here today, I think she'd even laugh about the time my sister locked her out of the house and that she therefore had to crawl back through a log pile chimney thing. Which doesn't sound right. I don't ever remember having a fireplace. But I remember that story.

My sister wasn't a four year-old racist. She was just a four year-old. And naughty. Yes, Mrs. Bell was every bit a part of my family, and her granddaughter was my earliest friend. My friend who once gave me a necklace she had made, but then got mad at me and asked for it back. I called her an Indian-giver. I had no idea what that meant, but later, again, learned that it was racist expression. I just remember not wanting to give the necklace back.

I'm lost in my thoughts again. Dancing words. Normal people call this a digression.

I listened to Lamott's book with my mouth wide open. (I would write "agape," but I can't remember if that means "love" or "open.") For, like, seven straight hours, I drove and I listened.

Sweet Jesus, did that woman just say the f-word again? Yes. Yes, she did.

And she talked about abortions and drugs and homelessness, and I kept wondering about her parents. Ridiculous. I know. But seriously, did her parents know she used the f-word? I had never heard anyone tell

That.

Much.

Truth.

Sometimes I get called naïve. I've also been called uptight, but I don't think that's important right now.

I might give you naïve. I might give you that forward-thinking politically liberal, socially conservative Christians living in a small predominately white town in the Bible Belt could possibly be naïve.

But being called naïve is annoying. And super offensive. Especially when you consider yourself incredibly worldly. As in full of world knowledge.

Reading this book made me feel, for the first time ever, naïve. Closed. Judgmental. It made me feel sick. Dirty.

Like I needed a shower. Not because of the stories that Lamott shared, but because of the stories that I hadn't lived. Not because of her truth or her language or her past. But because, in comparison, mine had been so …

So …

Come on, dancing words …

White.

Crisp. Clean. White.

Safe. Guarded. Protected. And the death-word for all of us would-be feminists, worse even than naïve —

Sheltered.

My world-view shifted. My atlas tilted.

Do atlases tilt? Mine did. Like I'd been tipped over. Like I'd been kicked on my ass. Except I can't say "ass" because while I'm not sure about Anne's mom, my mother is for sure reading this book.

Hearing truth. Unfiltered. Unashamed. If Lamott could say hard things out loud, could I? If she loved Jesus and asked hard questions and admitted being full-on crazy and broken, could I?

Nothing in her story mirrored my own, save for one. She loved Jesus. She spoke of the Jesus that I met as a young child, the Jesus who lived on the fringes and turned over tables in the synagogue and called out to the hypocrites, "Who among you will throw the first stone? Who among you is without sin?"

I sense the word of the Lord today is this: "Who among us will be the first to stop?" We are stoning our brothers and sisters. Sticks and stones? Break our bones? And words? They just break our hearts.

Who among us will be the first?

To stop.

When I first read Anne's admonition to write our stories, it was my ticket. A ticket to a tell all. I had stories. Hell yes, I did. And if people had wanted me to write warmly about them, then they should've treated me more kindly.

I write a blog about my life as a remarried, single mom and for a while, every time I posted a blog, we'd get a call from my new husband's ex-wife. The post that was most upsetting was one about her calling.

My husband.

All. The. Time.

PEARL

As Emma Claire would say, may I make a suggestion?

A humble suggestion for all my sisters out there. The single moms; the divorced moms; the ex-husband-has-remarried-after-you-left-him moms.

1. Don't watch The New Adventures of Old Christine.
2. Stay out of The Adventures of New Christine.
3. Don't call New Christine's husband.

I'd been given permission to tell my stories, but I'd also been given an incredibly generous and kind example of how to do so, by Anne Lamott.

Could I learn to do it well?

Could I learn from Anne? Could I say, "This is a big f-ing mess?" and say it well?

Could I share the story about opening a box that had been stored in our basement for years? Could I share the story about my ex-husband, the father of my children who at some point had to have loved me? Right? Could I share how that box shattered everything I thought I knew to be true?

The box. My ex-husband loved boxes. He loved organizing. He loved storage and shelves and he loved files and filing cabinets and sticky notes and packing tape. His boxes were more organized than most libraries; their contents carefully detailed with typed labels.

None of the typed labels read "Box full of gut wrenching truth that will make you feel like you've been kicked in the stomach, you ridiculously naïve, stupid, clueless woman." Truth is, the labels were printed on notecards, and I don't think all of that would've fit.

I did not ask for a divorce because I opened a box. I asked for a divorce and later happened upon the box. Anne has given me permission to tell my story, but the truth is that the contents of the box tell his. And his is not my story to tell.

When I was in high school, I entered the Miss De Queen High Pageant. Don't even. On stage, I was asked what person I would most like to meet. I said "Jesus."

No I didn't.

I said, "Arnold Schwarzenegger."

I wish I were kidding. In this life, we don't get do-overs. But oh, if we did. I would so do-over the Arnold answer.

I would also really love a do-over on the time I accidentally sent a very private, very descriptive Facebook message to the father of the man I was dating, instead of the actual man I was dating, but turned out not really to be dating, because apparently he had a live-in girlfriend.

(Dating after forty is wrong on so many levels. The real reason that God hates divorce is because He never wanted any of His children to have to experience dating after forty.)

Two things. First, we need to quit naming our sons after their fathers! This is just wrong. Maybe it used to be okay before social media. But no more.

Second thing. Don't send private Facebook messages full of rambling and way too much truth-telling unless you are certain that A. the intended recipient will receive the message instead of their Dad. And B. they don't already have a girlfriend!

Oh yes, I would love a do-over on that one. But we are not offered do-overs. Only do-betters. So today I would do it better.

Today I would choose to meet Anne Lamott. (And a boy without a girlfriend. Or a boyfriend.) Sorry, Arnold.

Traveling Mercies changed the way I saw my faith, my people, my story. *Traveling Mercies* took my black and white life, and colored me gray.

My feet are asleep. So is my brain. This is crazy. All this use of the f-word is incredibly draining. I need to go for a run. I need to sweat and breathe and work hard.

I take a nap instead.

And dream about Diet Coke.

The nap is short, but it'll do. I forge on.

> "You must do the thing you think you cannot do."
>
> ~ Eleanor Roosevelt

It's easy to wake up one morning and decide to live. It's quite another matter to do it. So I'm going to tell you something. Something that maybe nine people in the whole, wide, wack-a-do world (remember we're going to Mexico!) are going to believe.

God told me to get divorced.

PEARL

Yes. I already know. God hates divorce. But there, while running, at the corner of East Military Avenue and North Bell Street in Fremont, Nebraska, I heard Him speak.

"When are you going to do the hard thing I've called you to do?"

I did what any modern suburban mom would do. I tried pretending I hadn't heard Him. But I had.

The first person I told that Allen and I were broken was my sister. I remember that it was in her closet. Her beautiful closet that's bigger than my bedroom, with a crystal chandelier and a gorgeous wardrobe lined up by color. And season. (Who is this woman? And were we seriously spawned and raised by the same parents?)

Now, picture this. My closet is about twelve inches wide, just wide enough for the length of a hanger. You cannot walk inside. And the clothes are not separated by color. Or season. Some of them are on the floor.

(Thinking about my sister's closet reminds me why nobody believed my mother had gotten the goo from my sister's house, as opposed to the floor of my van. I think they were onto something.)

I hadn't planned to say anything to my sister about my marriage. I just blurted it out.

DAY THREE

I wish I could say I remember exactly what was said under the lights of her closet chandelier, but I don't. I just remember my sister being happy. Ya know, that I was sad. Well, rather that I was admitting to being sad.

Evidently, everyone knew but me.

"You've lost your effervescence," she said. And then she offered me money to retain an attorney.

I declined the offer, renewed my wedding vows alongside a river and vowed to try harder. Do better. I tried for another two years. I denied for another two years, and then I called my parents.

I had heard from the Lord. And this time I was listening. I was going into battle. Not a battle against my husband (yes, there was that, too) but a battle of obedience.

I was so courageous, y'all. Beating the love-warrior drum, I invited my husband to dinner. We met. We lovingly spoke of our marriage and our brokenness and I, with great courage and love, asked for a divorce.

Okay.

That is so.

Not.

What happened.

PEARL

Days and days passed; the words danced on; but I could not find my voice. I couldn't say the words out loud.

"When are you going to do the hard thing I've called you to do?"

Not today. Maybe tomorrow. Tomorrow's good. Day after that, even better.

I was scared. Scared of what people would say and what people would think and what people would say without taking time to think.

I was scared of hurting my husband's feelings. I know. Those are the dumbest words, ever. Hurting someone's feelings is when you forget to mention their new haircut.

"Honey, I don't mean to hurt your feelings, but I think we should get a divorce. I mean, maybe. Only if that's what YOU want. You know what? Never mind. I'm just tired."

Saying it out loud was the absolute scariest moment of my entire life. I also remember saying that I thought we could do it well. Like be poster parents for the whole divorced, co-parenting thing.

You wanna know something? You can't do it well. Even if you sorta-kinda do it well, it's horrible.

DAY THREE

I didn't leave for greener grass. My grass was dead. I left with a wounded spirit and a broken heart. My bones were tired from grief and the fire in my belly was snuffed out from years of watery tears. I felt less-than. Ugly. Embarrassed. Used-up. Left for walking-dead. And stuck. Like two pieces of paper glued together.

Ever tried gluing two pieces of paper together? Okay. I'll wait while you do it. Now, tear them apart. That's about as "well" as it gets when it comes to divorce. What a mess.

If you've been married twenty, thirty, forty years; if you've preached against divorce; if you've sat across from your sister-friend who's told you she's leaving her husband; if you've ever thought, how sad, how bad, how horrible for the kids; if you've ever in your holy life uttered the words, "God hates divorce:"

Let me just tell you something. We already know. You're gonna need some new material.

No, I didn't leave my husband in search of greener grass. I don't even like grass. Mowing makes me cry. Mowing is a man's job. (I told you I'm a feminist only when it's convenient. It has something to do with Eve eating the apple in the garden. Seriously. Look it up. It's right next to the passage about God hating divorce.)

I left my marriage in search of air. I needed to breathe.

PEARL

I did the hard thing I thought I could never do. I did it out of love for my children. I did it out of love for the father of my children. I did it out of radical self-care for myself. I did it out of obedience to a God who hates divorce but told me to do it anyway.

We must do the hard things we think we cannot do. We must wake up from our grief and rise up from our ashes and fight for joy and fight for air and breathe in His mercy and drink of His grace and remember that the grass isn't greener on the other side, but when you find yourself there:

Plant new grass. Water it. Watch it grow.

Then hire a man to mow it!

Monday, October 31, 2016

Speaking of grass, a wild marijuana plant grew in our yard all summer. Technically it was in our neighbor's yard but it's more fun to say that we are growing weed. Our dog sitter texted one day while we were on vacation and asked me if I'd seen the pot in the neighbor's yard.

I wrote back. Did we have a windstorm? How could our flowerpot blow into the next yard?

No. Not flower pot. Pot-pot.

Oh, yes. I joked. Mike and I are going to harvest it.

She then texted back with the dangers of smoking ditch weed, as I guess it's called in Nebraska.

I'm concerned that if she couldn't tell I was teasing about smoking wild weed that no one who reads this book will understand my humor either.

Maybe I'm not all that funny.

I bet smoking ditch weed from the neighbor's yard would be funny.

"The Good Thing Is."

~ Coulter

I was raised by incredibly optimistic parents.

"Earl has cancer. The good thing is, they caught it early and he'll be just fine. Well, maybe not totally fine; he might lose his arm, but the good thing is, they have terrific prosthetics these days."

"Johnny got three years in prison for dealing drugs, but the good thing is, now he can get clean."

"You didn't get that job? Great! That was a stupid job working with stupid people and this is a good thing."

DAY FOUR

My son, Coulter, has inherited this optimistic spirit. For his second birthday, his Uncle Gregory gave him a Little Tykes basketball hoop. Coulter would shoot the ball. Miss. And say, "Almost!" He would throw up the ball again. Miss again. And say, "Almost!"

This past summer he played on a competitive baseball team where he occasionally pitched. He's a good little athlete, but even he will admit that he either pitches fantastic, or he can't find the plate. In his defense, he is eleven.

He was pitching in a tournament. In tournaments, you must limit the number of innings a player can pitch. He walked player after player after player. Mercifully, his coach put him back at first base.

We won the game and advanced. We talked later about the rough inning.

"Yes! But the good thing is, since I didn't get any outs, it won't count as an inning."

The good thing is. There is always a good thing.

When Coulter was five, we would sneak up the back steps that led to our church. Coulter thought it was really cool that I had found this super-secret shortcut. He didn't know that the only reason we went that way was because I could never remember the little swipe card they used to check-in your children to Sunday school.

I sometimes struggle with the notion that rules apply to me. I never waited in a doctor's office until I was in my late twenties, and I still suffer from the idea that I have to wait with all the other sick people.

Life is cruel. And unfair.

One Sunday, right before we walked in, Coulter stopped suddenly and said, "Mom! Look! It's a robin's egg!" I looked down and there lay a cracked blue robin's egg and my heart sank. "Oh, Coulter! How sad. Mom's so sorry."

"Mah-ahm!" Coulter replied with confusion and frustration. "It's not sad. The baby bird cracked the egg and flew away. That's what they're supposed to do! It's a good thing!"

Well, duh! Yes, indeed!

This cracked egg is a good thing.

God says in His word that He will work all things together for good for those that love the Lord and have been called according to his purpose. Coulter, at two and five and eleven, is surely not quoting scripture, but he knows this Truth all the same.

DAY FOUR

The good thing is: There is always a good thing.

Because of God's redeeming grace, divorce and death and bankruptcy and homelessness and cancer and depression and adultery and addiction and all the broken pieces can be put back together. The cracks are gonna show. Sure. But that's how the light gets in. That's how the dark is made light. How the bad thing becomes good.

Okay, Lord, I get it. Somehow, in a matter of days, I went from writing so that my words would please You, to writing so that my words would impress others. Prove something to others.

I gave it to you, and now I feel myself taking it back.

It's like that time when I was trying to get pregnant and I finally just laid my heart bare and gave it all up to you. I opened my hands and said "Lord, this is yours. I open my hands and let go."

And then I found myself checking out of the local Barnes and Noble with a book called, *Taking Control of My Fertility.*

PEARL

Yes, Lord. This feels like that. I'll give you the book. I'll give you the words, but only if I can say exactly what I want about exactly who I want.

Okay, hands open, Lord. Give me the words.

> "... and I am out with lanterns, looking for myself."
>
> ~ The Letters of Emily Dickinson

Here are my best words from the hardest of times: Searching. Looking. Stumbling. Falling. Rising. Calling. Choosing.

I had chosen to dive, to jump, to leave. There was no room for doubt or fear or sadness or grief. Somewhere in the Sea of Separation, I decided that it didn't matter if I was okay, just as long as everyone thought I was okay. And if I wasn't okay, I had to pretend. Fake it till you make it, that sorta thing.

I was raising two children, had no job, and was sharing a home with their dad, from whom I was separated. It's called nesting.

DAY FOUR

Worst.

Idea.

Ever.

He refused to move out. I refused to move out.

Let's review. Men are supposed to mow the lawn. Men are supposed to support their families. When couples separate, men are supposed to move out!

It's not that hard. I realize that my mention of men mowing and supporting their families leaves my liberal-lady status in jeopardy, and I fully support your decision to mow your own lawn. I'm just saying that mowers are heavy. And they turn your shoes green. And if you forget to put oil in them, not because you forgot, exactly, but more like because you never knew you were supposed to, well, then the engine burns up.

Perhaps we should add mowing rights to the liberal agenda. As in, we have the right NOT TO MOW!

Nesting. It was going along fine (ish) until I was out of town interviewing for a job that, for the record, I was offered, but, again for the record, was not allowed to take. Something about a judge telling me I couldn't leave the state with my children.

PEARL

Again, with the rules and the laws.

My mom called me. "Now, don't get upset," she said. "I think this is actually a good thing. But I just wanted you to know that I threatened your husband with calling the police."

While watching my (okay, our) children in my (okay, our) home, Mother threatened to call the police on my husband for not going to the basement at the ordered time (we had a temporary agreement) and my husband, in turn, filed a restraining order against my mom.

Things were not okay. I was not okay. Nesting was

So.

Not.

Okay.

But you're surviving and you're trying to look normal, and you're trying to act like your children are completely fine because they have to be fine, otherwise the government-lady-never-married-mother-of-zero was right and you are definitely gonna screw up your children.

And you know what happens when you're trying to survive? You forget to grieve. Grieving the loss of someone still living. They don't send you flowers for that. Or food. Food would have been nice.

Next Pearl? I think we're on number eleven? When your friend gets divorced, make her a casserole. Something with cheese. And chocolate. A chocolate cheese casserole would be perfect. Perhaps with a perfectly paired side of vodka.

Yes. You forget to grieve. If I could make a timeline it would look something like this:

Year one: You pretend. Survive. Try to look normal.

Year two: You accidentally let a perfect stranger hug you at a party, and you've been so deprived of human touch for the past ten years that you actually say out loud, "Can you do that again?"

This man? He was the one with the unmentioned girlfriend and the dad with the same name. He, too, was out with the lanterns.

My husband finally moved out, and we began to move on, and at some point I remembered to grieve. I felt all the feelings that year. Hurt, anger, hope, joy. I laughed and cried and searched for the good things. I hugged strangers and tried to drink a margarita. (I was trying to act cool about it, but one of the ladies at the table caught me pouring sugar packets into my glass. Who knew that tequila was so bitter?)

Apparently, the sugar packets are just for your tea.

Here's what I learned: When you separate from your spouse, actually separate. When you leave town for a few days, do not leave your mother home alone with your soon to be ex-spouse. There may be police involved. And when you're searching for yourself, take up your lantern and search alone.

It's the only way back to yourself.

I'm trying really hard to forget that it's Halloween, but it's difficult when Eureka Springs seems to have an almost worshipful approach to the holiday.

Tucked into one of the most conservative regions in the country, the town has X-rated shops next to Christian boutiques, Diversity weekends and Drag Queen festivals. It's the perfect place for a socially conservative Christian who leans way left when it comes to politics, government, and social justice to write my story. I'm my very own paradox. My own Eureka Springs. I'm too conservative to be a liberal, and too liberal to be a conservative. Of course this is where I should tell my story.

Right now people are gathering from all over the tiny town for the annual costume parade. I've made plans to attend, but an introvert's favorite plans are cancelled ones, so I bail and go for a walk instead.

When I come back, refreshed, I dive back in . . .

> "Children are not a distraction from more important work. They are the most important work."
>
> ~ C.S. Lewis

This guy had the most captivating smile that I had ever seen. And the whitest teeth. Seriously. The dude had some ridiculously white teeth. As he preached, you could see them. All of them.

He had this way of looking right to you as if you were the only person in the room. He preached from the gospel of Mark. Told the story of friends who lowered their paralyzed brother through the roof to see Jesus.

He challenged us: Are you still captivated by the stories of Jesus?

PEARL

Am I?

Or I am held captive by circumstances and people and thoughts and fear?

And my children? Am I still captivated by them? I love them. I adore and cherish.

But am I captivated?

I remember this one day when the littles were littler. I had a complete nervous breakdown over the book, *Good Night Moon*. Was it a poem? Was it a book? What the Hell is this really about?

And what about *The Three Bears*? Seriously. Who cares? She ate your porridge and broke you chair. Get over it, you little crybaby. When you lose patience with Baby Bear, something is wrong.

And it wasn't just the books. It was the pretend play. Some days it's hard to feign interest in another Lego battle. "Yes, dear. Wonderful. I like what you've done with the sword. Oh. Not a sword? Well, dear, it's wonderful and what? His head came off? And they all died? You're kidding. That's wonderful, dear."

You see, we don't just build with Legos. We play with them. And in those fleeting, gory, bloodstained, dead

DAY FOUR

Lego-men moments that string together a life, am I still captivated? Or am I mad at Lego man for losing his head?

At bedtime, I have always been a single parent. In part, because I nursed my babies. I didn't want to quit nursing, because I loved that time at night when it could only be me. I was the only one they wanted. The only one they needed.

(I also didn't want to quit nursing because I could eat an entire pan of brownies in one sitting and not gain a single pound. American women who are nursing their five year-olds in a park are not doing it for the health of their children. They're afraid if they quit, their skinny jeans won't fit.)

But as the nursing moments came to a close, there were books. My mother read to us every night. Always. I have vivid memories of sitting on my bed listening and begging for her to read just one more story, one more chapter. To read, "'Now,' said she, 'we'll all have pancakes for supper,'" in a voice like Mrs. Bell's. Sorry, at the time we didn't know that *Little Black Sambo* was about an Indian child and not a little black Southern child. Besides, I don't think my mother speaking in an Indian accent would've had quite the same effect.

PEARL

"Just one more time," I'd beg. I wanted to create those same memories with my own children, and so bedtime was my thing.

During the process of divorcing my ex-husband, his brother sent a letter to the judge. It read: "She never gives them baths or reads to them."

Um. Am I living in crazy land? And how many times have you been in my home at bedtime?

Dumbass.

(I love the word "dumbass." It's my favorite line from *Legally Blonde*. After a lengthy legal explanation of common-law marriage and the issue of their dog, by Elle, the law student, Paulette, the hairdresser interrupts and says, "We're taking the dog. Dumbass!")

So. As a cranky side-note to my former brother-in-law: I've read to my children almost every night of their life, Dumbass!

Where was I? Yes. Cherished childhood memories.

Some nights I found myself, all snuggled together with two little blondies hanging on my arms, trying to hold a book in one hand and scratch itchy backs with the other, and I would read. But I wasn't captivated. And I wasn't present.

"Jack and Annie returned to the Magic Tree House and to their very great surprise, (how am I going to pay for health care?), there was a Dinosaur waiting at the end of the path (and where are we going to live?), but the Dinosaur was a plant-eater, so Annie became his friend, (and how could their mother have been such an idiot?), and they all lived happily ever after."

I was lost. And don't think for a minute that my children didn't know. They know when we are present.

Help me, Lord, to be present. Remind me that Coulter and Emma Claire are not a distraction from more important work. They are the important work.

Lego battles matter. The moon and the spoon and voices everywhere. They matter. Tossing the ball matters. Coloring outside the lines matters. Letting Emma Claire soak colored pencils in water because she learned from her friend, Elena, that it makes beautiful red lipstick, matters. And beautiful red lipstick is precisely what a captivated, ever-present smile needs.

Don't miss moments that matter. Don't miss the most important work.

Because that would pretty much be the dumbassiest thing we could ever do.

PEARL

Evidently the Halloween parade was quite fun (as the locals later shared) and for a brief moment I regret that I didn't take the opportunity to participate. But then I remembered that I don't like parades. Or people. But mostly, I don't like people in parades.

Or Halloween. I really don't like Halloween. I think it's weird to ask strangers for candy. I think it's weird for children to ask me for candy.

It's not that I haven't tried. When Coulter was two he wanted to be a football player for Halloween. Allen's mother tried to get him to wear a potato chip bowl with the big red University of Nebraska logo on it as his helmet. Instead, I bought a complete pint-sized Nebraska football costume for twenty dollars, and Allen's mother told me spending that much money on a Halloween costume for a two year-old was ridiculous.

Yes. Because wearing an upside-down potato-chip bowl on your head is not at all ridiculous.

My next attempt was the year Emma Claire was born. She was two weeks old on Halloween, and I was obsessed with dressing her up as a little piggy and dressing Coulter up as the Big Bad Wolf. If you dress your three year-old son up to look like he wants to eat his baby sister, can you chalk it up to post-natal hormones?

"Listen to the mustn'ts child. Listen to the don'ts.

Listen to the shouldn'ts, the impossibles, the won'ts.

Listen to the never haves then listen close to me.

Anything can happen child. Anything can be."

~ Shel Silverstein

Emma Claire, combing through her hair, looked up at me, as if to start in the middle of a conversation that wasn't actually taking place, and said, "It's not that you're not funny. I don't mean to be unkind. You are funny. Really. It's just that Dad's funnier. He lets us say funny words. Like butt-crack. Dad found a butt-crack in Coulter's pumpkin. And it was so funny. You don't think butt-crack's a funny word. So, ya know, that's why Dad's just a little bit funnier."

Yes. I know. Dad is hysterical.

Emma Claire continues, "Mom, what's that word when you have a lot of rules?"

PEARL

She thinks and thinks and finally it comes to her. "Strict! Daddy's not strict. He doesn't have rules."

And I wonder. What five-year-old knows the word "strict?"

She continues. "You make us use manners at the table, and we can't eat on the couch, and you make us say 'thank you,' and I'm not trying to be mean, Mom. You are fun. It's just that Dad doesn't . . ."

Coulter interrupts, always protective of his mother. "Mom's not strict."

"Thank you, Coulter," I interject. Wait. I should probably be a little bit strict, right? Little bit strict. Little bit fun?

Where's the balance? What's too much? What's not enough? And then I got a Word. I love getting a Word.

First Thessalonians. Being thankful in all things. We read it. I explain it to my children. You see, my children, it's not mom who's strict. It's not mom that expects you to say "thank you." I mean, I would totally be all cool with no rules and no manners, but dang it. What's a girl to do? I mean, it's God asking. Not me.

Their eyes were huge. They had walked straight into my trap, and I wish I'd had a microphone to drop. Because I'm that cool.

DAY FOUR

Boo-yah. I continue.

Ephesians. Honor your Father and Mother. Obey them in the Lord, for this is right. God has called us to honor — and obey.

I know, right? God again!

I care that we have fun. And I'll work harder at incorporating stupid butt-crack-type humor into my repertoire. But this manners and kindness thing … it's all on Jesus.

Not long after my promise to laugh at stupid jokes, I picked up Coulter and about eleven of his friends from school. I'm the queen of carpool. (I once used my mad carpooling skills on a leadership resume showing how I serve our community. I may have failed to mention that often the number of children exceeds the number of seatbelts. Because they don't. Because that would be wrong. And not at all safe.)

"Mom! Mom! You know how the science word for bottom is anus?"

Yes.

"Well today Mr. Hamilton said that "Uranus is not like other planets! Get it? Your anus?

PEARL

The eleven friends die laughing.

Coulter continued. "You know what else is funny? Blubber! Like a whale! Get it?"

More laughing.

Then it got weirdly quiet, and our buddy Cade said, "Wait. Where's my sister?"

Seriously? We forgot her?

Again?

I sent the kids back inside to find Cade's sister, but asked Coulter to stay behind. Serving another family had called for changing some pretty big plans for the following week, and I knew he would be disappointed.

I explained about serving and sacrificing and loving and then I pulled the God-thing on him again.

"This is what Christians do. We love others."

He was quiet. Then he replied, "Oh. I thought we were Presbyterian."

So right there, in the carpool line, I laid it out. Theology, Jesus, denominations, Protestants, Catholics, you name it. We covered it. Again, I wish I'd had a mic. Nailed it.

He looked at me. This is a moment I will remember forever.

"Mom. I didn't eat my Fruit Gushers today. I decided to save them. And by the way, you totally forgot to pack a spoon, and I had to get a spoon from the cafeteria, and I'm pretty sure that they don't clean the dishes in there. It was wet and gross, and I've been in that place a lot and I've never even seen a dishwasher."

Okay, baby. Tomorrow I will pack spoons. Tomorrow I will remember Cade's sister before I drive away. Tomorrow I will laugh when you figure out that "European" is also funny.

Tomorrow. Anything can happen, child. Anything can be.

It's funny, how clear my thoughts become with distance. Not simply the miles that currently separate, but the years as well. I know I should be homesick.

I'm not.

Again, it's a discipline more than anything. I've been given a gift and I will not waste it.

PEARL

Tennessee Williams wrote *A Streetcar Named Desire*, set in New Orleans, while living in a hotel in Key West. Emily Dickinson wrote enduring poems about the natural world while a recluse in the family homestead in Amherst. Maybe this enforced distance is part of what Virginia Woolf meant when she said every woman needs a room of her own.

For the record, I've read none of the above, because I'm not smart like that, but as I cherish my week as a recluse it's fun to think that I have so much in common with Emily Dickinson and Virginia Woolf.

This is a room of my own, for three more days. Use me, Lord. Help me to capture the dancing words.

> "God never withholds from His child
> that which His love and wisdom call good.
> He never denies us our hearts' desires,
> except to give us something better.
> His denials are always merciful."
> ~ Elisabeth Elliot

Enter my husband. No. Not that one. The new one.

At precisely the same time that a judge was (mercifully) denying my request for removal from the state; at precisely the same time the judge said "no," over and over again; at precisely the same that a judge, this king of Fremont as it were, sitting on his throne, declared Allen and me "irrevocably broken," God gave me Mike.

Which totally sounds like a country and western song title. I'm on the writer's clock. I must not get distracted and believe that I can write lyrics to a country song about Mike.

Dancing words, be still!

I had been separated two years before I met Mike. We dated (which is a super strange word when you're talking about two middle-aged people. Except let it be known that I don't consider forty-four to be middle-aged. Mike, on the other hand, is probably there.)

On our first date, my soon-to-be husband took me to an outdoor concert. In his version of the story I talked the entire time. I find this difficult to believe. (No one else does.) In his version of the story, I spilled out the past three years of my life while sitting in a lawn chair listening to a cover band. Again, difficult to believe. And may I remind you who is closer to middle age?

The year that followed, we didn't so much date, as we filled our empty hours, our empty spaces with each other.

PEARL

Divorce is a death, made all the more agonizing because our culture doesn't recognize it as such. And to grieve a person that is still living? It will break your heart.

Right.

In.

Two.

A widowed mother is never alone to grieve. A widowed-by-divorce mother who's sharing custody with the living man that she's still grieving, is alone. Far too often.

The Lord brought Mike into my life, and together we grieved, and together we healed. We filled up empty spaces and empty hours and, three years after my separation, after one year of completely being on my own, he asked me to marry him.

This was not a surprise. I knew he had the ring. I knew he was waiting for the perfect moment. I knew he was trying the whole romance thing and I was just like — DO IT ALREADY!

I wanted the world to know. I was loved. I was lovely and lovable and worthy of love and yes, I wanted everyone to know.

Some people thought it was too fast. (Did I mention the middle aged thing?) Some people thought it would be too hard. (Three divorces, three ex-spouses, six children, and two grandchildren.) They were right.

I remember being asked, "Don't you want to be single for while? Do it on your own? Prove something to yourself? Prove yourself to others? Don't you want to do the whole strong-single-momma thing?"

This was fair and appropriate and right. It was right to question. I had been not-okay for so long, how could anyone close to me think that I was ready to do the whole broken-blended thing?

I vividly remember telling my Mother three things.

1. I will never get married again. Like, ever.

2. But if I do get married (and I'm not going to), he will have crazy money. Like, serious money. Old money. (None of this tacky nouveau riche thing.) I've married for love and that didn't work, so next time around it'll be for money.

3. He will be my age, and not have any children, but if he does have children, they will have to be between the ages of six and nine, so as not to mess with Coulter and Emma Claire's birth order.

PEARL

But as I look back on my journals and remember the cries of my heart, I prayed for none of those things. Seriously y'all. How could I forget to pray for the money thing?

Instead, I prayed for a kind man who loved Jesus and would be kind to me and my children. A generous man who would be a strong head of our family (sorry, liberal ladies) and lead us in the blending. I prayed for a loving man who would adore me and adore my children and ultimately offer an example to Coulter and Emma Claire on what a good and holy marriage should look like.

I prayed for all of that. And I forgot the money. It must be the age thing.

I already had, by the way. (I'm back to the original question.) I had already been a strong single momma long before I signed divorce papers. And now, I wanted a husband.

God's refusals are always merciful. He never denies our hearts' desires except to give us something better. And this, y'all? This loving? This blending? This crazy hard puzzle that feels like a piece is always missing?

So.

Much.

Better.

Tuesday, November 1, 2016

For breakfast this morning I ate leftover meringue bones (a delicious nod to Halloween) served last night by Jana, our incredibly talented chef here at the Writers' Colony. Every night she wows the writers with her gourmet meals.

For the record, I also had oatmeal. It felt like the right thing to do. It occurs to me that even if I'd remembered my yoga pants, I'd be out of luck. There's no amount of stretch that would account for the fact that I've added leftover dessert to my breakfast ritual.

Waiting for the oatmeal, I found myself sharing life stories with Jana, and it's possible I complained about following a man to Nebraska and how I've been homesick my entire adult life with my family so far away in Arkansas. She smiled, and in her sweet accent said, "Yes, Yes. I understand, child. My family lives in the Czech Republic."

Yeah. So. Czech Republic. Nebraska. Pretty much the same, right?

"It was rather beautiful: the way he put her insecurities to sleep. The way he dove into her eyes and starved all the fears and tasted all the dreams she kept coiled beneath her bones."
~ Christopher Poindexter

It was rather beautiful, the way he taught her to breathe. As if along the way, she had forgotten. The way he loved even her most unlovely parts.

It was rather beautiful, the way he spoke love in all her languages and sat patiently with her in the dark. How they sat together in her sad places.

It was rather beautiful, the way he let her have her way, her fits, her rushing temper, her tantrums, and how he never quieted her. To quiet her would dim the flame and dull her spark.

Beautiful.

Because, as he starved her fears, he fed her soul. As he tasted her dreams, he said these are good. And right. Go chase them, my love. Run fast, and dream.

Your insecurities are sleeping, and I will keep a night watch. And unlike the girl in her mirror, he didn't see a frightened child needing to be saved. He saw a fiery and spirited woman trying to be brave.

It was rather beautiful, how their love affair began in the furnace. Born of betrayal. Born in ashes of shame.

But this love, this affair of mercy and goodness and grace and love, God what a love, does not end in the ashes.

And that, my love, is a rather beautiful thing.

For a while, I'm lost in memories of Mike. I find myself marveling at the mysteries of our great God and trying to imagine my life before him. Which really isn't that hard since I'm surrounded by journals reminding me of just that life.

But then I remember I'm almost out of days here, and a book won't write itself, even if you've made yourself a pencil in the hand of God.

Which reminds me, I bought a pencil for Coulter today, made out of bark supposedly from a tree here in the Ozarks. I thought it would be special. A writing tool from my writing retreat.

Who am I kidding? I got played. That pencil was totally made in some Chinese factory, wasn't it?

"Leadership is not about being in charge.
Leadership is taking care of those in your charge."
~ Simon Sinek

This summer I applied for a leadership program through the Chamber of Commerce. This was a ridiculous decision, because I don't like meetings. I don't like networking. And, well. I don't really like people.

Except you. You bought my book. I like you.

It was education day. We heard from community leaders. We took a super fun tour of the University that holds the final memories of my marriage. I held back tears. And vomit.

We were given handouts that boasted of scores and dollars and technology. And assessments and new assessments and better assessments.

"What does A-B-C really mean anyway? It's confusing for parents." Really? Because I'm pretty sure I understood it. We've had a new grading system in Fremont every year for the past five years. Every. Dang. Year.

Last week I opened Coulter's report card.

A.

A.

A.

4 (the non-confusing way to say "A.")

3 (The non-confusing way of saying I need to talk to Coulter about spraying water bottles in class.)

1 (The non-confusing way of saying that Coulter is performing below grade level in Writing. Back in the day, this was called an "F.")

Except that's impossible.

I emailed his teacher to schedule a meeting. Either there had been a huge mistake, or someone was about to lose his phone. And freedom.

The teacher's reply:

"Coulter has a ninety seven percent. Unfortunately, we are still tweaking the grading system. It's like putting a round peg into a square hole."

What the Hole? How round was that peg? Wait. I think it was square. Yes. That makes more sense. See? It makes you crazy.

I miss the grading from the eighties. The one that was grounded in basic mathematical equations. (Michael Jackson would be so sad.)

We can change grading, implement new policies, test more, test harder, test better, and none of it will ever matter unless my kindergarten teacher, Mrs. Reigner, matters. Unless Margaret Turner matters. Unless Jane Harding, who flipped a switch in my brain that could never be un-switched, matters.

And Bobby Holcombe, my senior English teacher, who taught me a love of reading; who sent me the most precious piece of mail I've ever received. It read: "It's not the crown that makes the princess."

But, dang it, I'd really wanted that crown.

Bill Blackwood, who opened his home night after night to tutor us in algebra. We'd crunch on Werther's Original hard candies and do math.

Rosemary Jones. Nancy Copeland. Unless our teachers matter, nothing matters.

Y'all! This is easy.

At forty-four, high school memories fade fast, but I remember my teachers. It's not numbers. It's community. It's not curriculum. It's relationships. It's about investing in our teachers so that they invest in our children.

And now let's talk about prayer in schools. Just kidding.

(Before I decided to solve the education crisis in our country, I was telling you about the Leadership program.)

It required an application. Community groups. Leadership positions. Local boards. Sure. Right. Well. Let's see.

There was nothing. My mind was as blank as the page. I wept.

PEARL

I haven't been "on salary" since I was twenty-seven. I have lived an incredible life hour by hour, earning my way. And I have worked hard. Not digging ditches, building bridges hard, but "manicure intact" hard.

When my ex-husband Allen and I first moved to Nebraska (where we currently and separately are raising our children), people assumed I was a stay-at-home mom. No. I was an unemployed mom. (Reminded daily by my husband of the financial burden that I was placing on our family.)

So I'm staring at this page. Trying to think of a time in my life when I would've had time to join a group. When I wasn't working. That hour. And the next hour.

My parents were community leaders. My siblings. My friends. My ex-husband. But I had nothing.

I recently confided to a friend a long-held dream to sing the National Anthem at an Arkansas Razorbacks football game. My friend joked, "Yeah, right. And now, to sing the National Anthem, here's your very own Miss Nebraska!" (A different book. A different life.)

"They don't have to announce that I was Miss Nebraska," I said.

His reply?

"What else have you done?"

Yes. In the past twenty years, what else have I done? Looking at this application, apparently nothing. Nothing worthy of singing the National Anthem, anyway.

Sisters, here's what I know. Life is not about building a resume. I've made peace with my empty application. Seriously. Sorta. I will. Eventually.

If I had to do it again, this is what I'd write:

"I'm a mom. By God's miraculous design, I grew babies. Inside my body."

I know, right?

First baby. My water broke. We went to the hospital. You know what happens when your water breaks at home? Or, better still, in your husband's car? They don't believe you. They want to check. As if the breaking of water could be confusing.

Here's how it goes. They bring in their youngest nurse. She's the standard age for nurses - twelve. An older, more experienced nurse hands her a giant fork-like tool-thingy. Mercy! I just had to choose a teaching hospital. Giant fork-like tool-thingy goes inside, up into parts unknown, and then she cranks it. You know when you're changing a tire, and you crank the jack to raise the car higher and higher? Yes. It was like that. A giant car jack.

(That example came from the sky because I have never in my life changed a tire. Another case of selective feminism. Changing tires is for men.)

It was like an episode from Will and Grace. She looks for a vein in which to start antibiotics. (I had some issue that required antibiotics. I forget what.) She can't find a vein. And the next nurse can't find one. Nor the nurse after that.

Finally they decide on the vein in my hand. This is at 4:00 p.m. on a Sunday. Coulter was born, sans drugs, around 10:00 p.m. on Monday night. I said MONDAY night, y'all!

The following morning a doctor with the personality of a rock told us that Coulter may or may not die (Good morning, new parents!), and was taken into the ICU, where his veins also proved stubborn.

They gave him his first haircut and put the needle into his head. I have never cried harder. By God's great Mercy, Coulter did not die. We left on Friday. Alone.

Allen had sent my parents back to Arkansas. Evidently this was just about "us".

That night, in the dark, I nursed my baby and wiped scared, salty tears. I knew two things.

I had never been more grateful.

And.

I had never been more scared. My marriage was in trouble.

It would be six more years, two pregnancies, one miscarriage and one miraculous Emma Claire later that I would actually dive into the "Sea of Affliction", but that night, I knew.

I totally forgot where I was going with this whole leadership thing. But my point is this.

I had a baby. I broke all the blood vessels in my face during delivery, looked like I had the measles, and when Coulter was two days old, I met a woman in the hall who said, "Oh! Looks like someone is getting ready to have a baby."

Except someone had ALREADY had a baby.

I didn't hit her. I didn't hit the doctor who forgot to say good morning before telling me that my son might die, and I didn't hit my husband who had told my parents to leave.

PEARL

That's leadership, yes? Well, maybe not, but it's still pretty dang impressive.

It's time to update our applications! I'm a mom. I'm leading a family, and while it doesn't make for a sparkling resume, I'm pretty sure you want me to do a good job. You know, because of the whole "children are our future" thing.

Next week is our leadership class graduation. I think I'm the only person not graduating "with honors."

Evidently you can only miss a half day over the entire year to be considered for honors. I'm sorry; do you know how hard it is to sit in meetings? All day? With people?

Well, you probably do. But it's crazy hard. And I like naps. And not being in meetings. And not being with people.

I also really like awards, though, so next week at graduation, I'm going to be pretty sad.

If only they'd come up with a "you pushed a seven-pound human out of your body, and now you drive around lots of seventy pound humans, and while you may have threatened to shoot Nerf-gun bullets at the carpool bullies, you never actually did it, and for that we are so proud of you" award. Yes. There should definitely be a trophy for that!

Recently, Mike I were traveling and I'd forgotten to bring my medicine. I take a little something I call my, "the world is not ending; you are not dying; and this is not a crisis" pill. And I take it every day. But we'd been down to visit family in Arkansas, and I'd forgotten.

Three full days.

When someone does something crazy on the news, or when my ex-wife-in-law (that's my husband's ex-wife) says something ugly, I just think, "Somebody's gone off their meds."

Or maybe it's just that their hearts are ugly and bitter. Yes. It's one of those two things. And for the record, I have no idea if anyone in our immediate or ex or extended family is on meds. Except for me. And this trip, I was off my meds.

The third night, I actually remembered, but was too tired to get up and do anything about it. I rolled over in bed and nudged my husband. "If I threaten to leave you tomorrow, Baby, it's because I forgot my 'life's not over' pills."

He said, "Okay. Good to know."

And I didn't threaten divorce, but I did act like a three year-old who didn't get to be line leader for the day.

PEARL

We were driving back to Nebraska. My dad had suffered a major medical trauma, so I didn't want to leave Arkansas. I was mad at my ex-husband for the whole "Nebraska" thing, and evidently I was upset that my sister-in-law was receiving an award.

I love my sister-in-law just like I love my husband, and wasn't really planning to leave him, so before you judge me too harshly, please review the opening paragraphs. My sister-in-law is incredibly intelligent and beautiful and accomplished and most definitely worthy of awards.

And yet, I cried.

Why does she always get awards? Why do I never get any awards? What about an award for carpooling every day? What about that? What about an award for letting your children play with Play-Doh and use paint without drop cloths and make 'from your head' recipes that involve flour? Lots and lots of flour.

What about not going to prison for murder? Staying out of jail post-separation? That deserves a big ol' award!

(I'm just kidding. That was not a threat on anyone's life. I would never hurt anyone. Unless you hurt my children and then it's gloves off. Or is it gloves on? Anyway, orange is not my color.)

DAY FIVE

My husband Mike is incredibly generous during these fits. He lets the crazy fully run its course. He knows me far beyond what our number of years together would suggest.

About three hours after our wedding, I told him that we had made a terrible mistake. One week later, I told him the same thing. Again at two months and six months, and it was probably almost a full year after our wedding before I quit saying (or thinking) that we had made the stupidest decision in the history of forever.

Second marriages are harder than first marriages. Sorry. Look it up. Harder still? Third marriages. We have like an eight percent chance.

I've decided the only way this marriage will work is if both his ex-wife and I stay on our meds. It's not an "either or." It's a "both and."

Again with the humor. (My lawyer will want me to say this.) I have no idea if Mike's ex-wife is on any sort of medication. Only that, if not, she should be.

Depression or mental illness is obviously not funny, but when you're the third wife in a cracked-up triangle, when you're down deep searching for pearls, humor is oxygen.

As soon as we got home, Mike gently suggested I take my medicine, which I thought was a good choice, so I did, and then I took a nap, and then I was very happy for my sister-in-law.

For some reason, Coulter knows this story. I think he overheard me telling a friend about my ridiculous outburst. A week later, Coulter and I were given the gift of a trip to New York City. (It was supposed to have been my parents' trip, but my dad was still in the hospital.) The conversation leading up to the trip went a little something like this.

Me: "Mother, we need to cancel the trip."

Mother: "We are not cancelling the trip."

Me: "Really, Mother, we need to cancel the trip."

Mother: "We are not cancelling the trip."

I called the airline to transfer the tickets into my name, since Coulter and I were now going, instead of Coulter and my parents.

Me: "I need to transfer a ticket to my name."

Airline Operator: "That's impossible. It's a non-transferable ticket."

Mother (taking the phone from my hand): "I need to speak to your boss. And her boss. And that person's boss."

DAY FIVE

Shall I continue? The tickets were transferred, and Coulter and I went to New York City.

I try so hard to pack well. Even for this trip to the Writers' Colony, where everything was provided, I forgot things. I even made a list. And checked it. Never. I never checked it.

I brought a blanket, but forgot my pillow. The pillows here remind me of very old pancakes. I brought a toothbrush, but not toothpaste, and I brought my favorite pair of yoga pants to write in; only when I unfolded them, they were Emma Claire's. I brought Emma Claire's favorite yoga pants.

Similar things happened on the New York City trip. I said to Coulter, "Oh my gosh. I'm so sorry. If they gave out awards for the worst packer in America, I would win!"

Coulter smiled. "Well, the good thing is, that's one award Aunt Mica won't win."

God, I love that kid. And his Aunt Mica.

So I started this day determined to write about Mike, and ended up writing about a vacation trip with Coulter. Does this make me a good momma, or one of those helicopter parents too obsessed with every little detail of their children's lives? No. I'm not a helicopter mom.

Helicopter moms do not forget to offer their children breakfast before school. They don't find said breakfast by scrounging through the backseat of their car.

I mean, backseat of their lemon.

They also don't forget to pick up their children from school.

These are random examples, of course.

Hmm. I wonder if I have any snacks in the back of the rental car? No. I need to write. I'm sure if I focus, I can come up with a few more examples that will exclude me from the Mom of the Year club.

"That's the lesson of life, isn't it? It gives us one person who both shows us that true love exists and that fairy tales don't."

~ Leo Christopher

It will go down as the day I killed the Easter bunny. And along with it, fairytales.

I suck.

Yes. I outed the Easter Bunny. I felt pretty good about it at first. Confident. Parenting at its finest. And then less so. Guilty and completely paranoid that I'd crushed Emma Claire's imagination, and stolen a piece of her childhood.

But come on, y'all. A Bunny that hops from home to home delivering baskets? Flying reindeer, yes. This of course makes sense, but long-distance marathon bunnies? Laying eggs?

This is Easter. I cannot think about bunnies. Unless the bunny has been crucified. And is coming back to life. To save, you know, all of humankind.

Single parenting is hard. Single parenting during holidays is super-hard, and I've gotta tell you, I'm stone-cold weary of pretend-characters stealing all the glory.

My glory.

I suppose I should also be concerned that they're taking a little glory away from Jesus, as well. Yes. Probably.

I'm not a Grinch.

PEARL

I filled baskets. Fun baskets. Emma Claire's basket had beautiful rocks (because for some reason, rocks, and I quote, are "very special" to her) and I filled them with Nerf guns and water guns and Emma Claire got her own, because I know how upset she gets when she's left out of "boy" games, and there was candy and a really cool water bottle, and she woke up Sunday morning, sprang out of bed and ran to find her basket.

And there was joy.

But after church, after the Resurrection celebration, Emma Claire came home and complained that the Easter Bunny didn't bring very much.

Coulter defended him, defended me. "Emma Claire, yes he did. He brought a lot."

Half an hour later, tears welled up into her eyes, and her grief continued. "Mom. YOU forgot to give us anything for Easter."

I learned recently to always respond "to emotion with emotion." So, instead of giving her the whole, "Easter is not about you getting gifts" mom-answer, I pulled her onto my lap and said, "Emma Claire, can I tell you a secret? The Easter Bunny did not leave this basket for you. Easter is about Jesus, and the bunny is just a fun, silly way to celebrate spring. The Easter bunny doesn't know that rocks are special to you. And the Easter bunny doesn't know how you like to have your own Nerf gun. Your mom knows."

She looked up at me, completely unimpressed that I was the thoughtful gift-giver, and says, "Oh. Okay. Is Santa Claus real?"

I answered honestly. "Well, duh! Yes! Who else would drive the sleigh?"

Just kidding.

"Yes. Santa will still come. He will come because he brings gifts to celebrate Jesus' birthday, but Easter is nobody's birthday."

She hopped off my lap. "Okay, Mom, but I may want to talk about this again later."

Sure thing, Emma Claire. My lap is always open.

I don't know if I did the right thing. It was selfish and self-serving. And true and hard. All I know is, when she thought that I had forgotten her, I needed her to know that I hadn't.

And I would never forget her.

Well, except at church. I did forget her there.

PEARL

But only once.

I also forgot my friend's daughter at school. You remember Cade's sister, yes? So yes, sometimes I forget. But, do you know what I will never forget?

I will never forget the look on Emma Claire's face when she realized it was her mom who had gotten her those special rocks.

And I will never forget her meticulously placing them, one-by-one into a vase for safe keeping.

And I will never forget Coulter coming upstairs with a Star Wars Lego man hanging from a Lego cross with Lego chains and a spear in his side because, "Do you remember, Mom? That's how they checked to see if Jesus was really dead."

Yes, Coulter. I remember.

And that's the way with life. It gives us one person to show us that true love exists, and because of that, we don't need fairytales. God gave us mothers.

Two more days.

I stare out the window at the view I've come to love, and recognize that the clock is ticking on my time here. I began to dread the drive home, knowing that with each mile north I'll leave the beauty that is October behind me and drive right into November.

Winter.

It feels like failure out there.

I feel like a failure.

Who in their right mind tries to write a book in a week?

"What's the difference between a Midwestern fairytale and a Southern fairytale? A Midwestern fairytale begins with "Once upon a Time." A Southern fairytale begins with "You're not gonna believe this shit!"

~ Origin Unknown

PEARL

That's what this day felt like. Gather 'round friends. Gather 'round family. You're not gonna believe this shit.

We were at the kitchen table. God's grace is never closer than at a kitchen table. Where truth spills out over biscuits and bacon. Where tears and sweet tea and barbecue run together.

In the South, we gather. Brandon Hatmaker says, "There is no better place for a friend or neighbor to first hear the gospel than in our living rooms or at our dinner tables."

At the kitchen table, we sit. We eat. We fellowship.

The legacy of my Grandmother Pearl is so strong that even though she's been gone many, many years, her children return. And when her children passed, her children's children returned. To her table.

On this occasion, the passing of my Aunt Ann, we were all there. The first time in almost forty years that all the Coulter cousins were together, gathered around the kitchen table. We shared our stories, our memories, and our hearts.

Over food, obviously. This is the South.

It happened slowly. One cousin asked. Another joined in. Hearts open. Listening. We went from grieving the dead to caring for the living.

I answered. Quietly at first. Through the years, I had lived my faith loud, and worn it like a brightly colored coat. There was so much shame. Humiliation. Me. The little Jesus-lover who failed in the one way Christians must never fail. Me. The little Jesus-lover whose marriage should've lasted, but didn't.

I wanted more than anything to share the gospel. At this moment. Around this table. I wanted to witness that God is still good. He is faithful. He is kind.

People break vows, but God never will. People make promises. God keeps them.

Aunt Betty walked over, dragging her oxygen tank, and sang out, "Yes! Please talk to us. Your Mother won't tell us a damn thing."

We laughed. Laughter through tears. Nothin' better.

Before long, I had shared the whole shitty tale, and do you know that not one person said, "God hates divorce?" Not one person asked me if I had tried counseling. They didn't say anything. They just listened.

To my story.

To my life.

PEARL

There are not, in fact, two sides to every story. People tell you that, but it's a lie. It's their way of saying they don't believe you.

"Well, you know, Marge, there's two sides to every story."

No. Dumbass, there's not.

There's just the one. Just yours. Just mine. Just truth.

And the truth is that sweet, Christian, little Myra Katherine, who's been a Jesus-lover since the eighties, is now a divorced mom.

I know that Jesus is bigger than divorce. I know that what my children need more than married parents is a loving God. I know that Jesus is on my side. His story counts for mine. His truth counts for mine.

And that's no fairy tale.

Day Six

Wednesday, November 2, 2016

Last night, I carried that good ol' family feeling right into the Writers' Colony dining room with me. Another table filled with like-minded people. Another set of folks willing to listen and understand, if only I'd open up and be honest. Another family — this one of writers — ready to take me in and love me up.

I know you'll find this hard to believe, but I talked for the entire first course. I told my fellow writers I was terrified of not producing a book, after I'd told everyone where I was going and what I was doing, and after my family had been so supportive.

I told them the whole messy story of my marriage and divorce and re-marriage. I told them that while they'd been publishing their work, I'd been looking for work. I told them that while they were tossing bad first drafts in the trash, I was tossing diapers.

I told them the truth. I'm afraid that, rather than being a pencil in God's hand, I might just be a hack, a pretender, a fraud. I sometimes feel like I'm one truth away from people seeing the real me.

Then I inhaled.

Now it was their turn. A writer, poet, mother said, "Read us something."

"What?"

"Read to us."

And so I did.

And when I looked up from my screen, she was crying.

"You have a story to tell, my friend. Tell it."

I walked away tonight realizing that all of us here has the Imposter Syndrome. We are all in the fake-it-till-you-make-it club.

Jana is a gourmet chef but she doesn't stick around for clean-up. So we gathered our dishes and cleaned our plates and opened our hearts. I left feeling encouraged and hopeful.

If nothing else happens, I came. I met new people and I wrote and I didn't die.

"Love is the bridge between you and everything."

~ Rumi

Looking back, I can't say for sure how my children felt about my upcoming marriage.

Scientists believe that when it comes to grief, your children are about a year behind you. Sometimes more. Mike and I bought a house, and it nauseates me to remember how I used the house to bribe them into excitement over the marriage. It was my dream house. But not theirs.

You know you are making crazy hard decisions that will impact your children forever, and will impact the adults they become and the relationships they form, and it's paralyzing. Like in a horror movie, when you know you should be running, but you're too scared to move. I knew I was being faithful. I knew I was choosing their best. And if I could trust the Lord to bring Mike to me, I would have to trust the Lord to bring Mike to my kids.

PEARL

My children loved Mike instantly. That was never the problem. But marriage. There's a finality to it. There's grief.

"Mom? Does this mean you can't marry daddy again?" asked Emma Claire.

"Yes, dear. That's what it means."

Broken families. Broken hearts.

I heard an author put it this way: When you get married and you say vows and you make promises, it is a covenant between you and God and your spouse and yes, when you get married, it is like super-gluing together two pieces of paper. And then, divorce. You tear those papers apart. What a hot mess!

I want to take two pieces of paper and I want Emma Claire to see just how impossible it would be to put those pieces back together. But I don't. I tell her she's too young to understand.

It's true, I think. How could I ever explain the glue and the paper and the vows and the broken promises and she is — they both are — too young. But the look on her face told me something different. And silently I committed to never say that again.

It's lazy. A cop-out. And I'm done being lazy.

But what do I want her to see? Others to see? Not just how impossible it would be to put the pieces back together, but just how impossible it was to separate them in the first place. Again, what a crumpled hot mess.

Remember the story of my sixty-five year-old mother, as she untangled, unpretzeled herself from the floor of my mini-van at Six Flags, and noticed that her bottom was sticky?

We don't have time for a full bio on my Mother, but I'll give you a picture.

Sally Fields. *Steel Magnolias.*

So when you wonder why the day couldn't proceed as planned, just because of a little sticky goo, then ask yourself, would M'Lynn have gone to Six Flags with goo?

No. No she would not.

You'll recall that we found the nearest ladies room and my mother hid in the stall while my sister and I washed and rubbed and scrubbed and dried and finally got the goo out, but found we'd rubbed a quarter-size hole into the seat of my mother's pants.

Divorce is like sitting in putty. You can get it out, but you'll be left with a hole. And there is nothing, in all the history of the world, that will ever fill it.

Anyway.

Instead of waiting for my next chance, my next opportunity to not blow it with a "you're too young" moment, I decided to create it. I asked the kids if they wanted to jump on the trampoline.

It's hard work, because Coulter makes up ridiculously elaborate rules, and you must follow them. You must throw a ball, then catch it, and then do a cannon ball, and then re-throw it, and I lost the game, of course, probably because I never really understood how the points were made.

"Coulter," I said. "This is a little random."

He looks at me like it's not at all surprising that I would say something random, and I proceeded to tell him that he can ask me anything he wants, and I will never answer by telling him he's too young to understand.

He is young.

And it is hard.

But so is math. And so is reading. And so is the Creation Story. And yet, somehow, we find a way to teach it.

DAY SIX

Every year, my children hear the story of the virgin Mary, and every year we talk about the birth of Jesus, and we teach Jesus as the Son of God and yet fully God and oh, by the way he was nailed to a cross and they put him in a tomb and then he woke up and he rose up and he reigns and we can believe in His name and we can call on His name and we are living in a Good Friday world, waiting for our Easter Sunday, and what a hypocrite!

I expect my children to understand this? Believe all of this, and yet I can't figure out a way to explain divorce?

In fancy divorce books, probably written by the government lady who'd never been married and never had children, you'll read that all kids need is to be loved. Really? Is that all they need?

Or do they need shoes and books and soccer cleats and baseball pants?

Just love?

Or do they need to hear about the paper and the goo and the promises torn in two?

Coulter and Emma Claire's first understanding of promises, and broken ones at that, came from the two people they trusted most. How can they learn to trust in the promises of God, if they can't even trust in the promises of a parent? How can they trust in love?

Recently I was sharing my divorce story, and a man stops me and says, "Oh, are you a new Christian?"

It's time like this when I must decide. Take a deep breath or throat punch him?

As if "old" Christians can't get divorced.

Nope.

Found Jesus. Have had Jesus. Have always known Jesus. Got divorced anyway.

And since I didn't really know him, (the man, not Jesus), I decided to leave out the part where I heard the voice of the Lord at the corner of Military and Bell asking me when I was going to do "the hard thing that He had called me to do." Some people don't believe that the voice of the Lord will tell you to get divorced.

Death and divorce force this weird rearranging of sorts and creates a dynamic which, left unchecked, give children more power and more authority than they should have. This was the single hardest concept for me to grab hold of.

I didn't ask my two-year-old if I should get divorced. I trusted in a good and merciful God.

And so, while we must respect and protect and absolutely make decisions that are the best decisions for our children, I'd have to ultimately decide that it was not good and not right to, in turn, ask my five year-old if I should get married.

It's too heavy. What child needs that brick on their shoulders? This was my mountain, not theirs. I would climb it. And with help from arms stronger than mine, I would carry them up. Together.

All they need is to be loved?

No. They need to KNOW they are loved. They need to be shown love. They need parents who don't put their children first, but put their children best. They need a village circling, showering, raining down Christ's love so that it might carry them across the bridge from broken to whole.

Build the bridge. Build it with love. Then hold their hands as you walk them across.

PEARL

Getting numb-tush again. And what I'm now calling "writer's back." Lord-a-mercy, my back hurts. Occupational hazard of writers, I suppose. I do a few yoga stretches, and carry on.

> "So enchanted with you were the wind and the rain that they whispered the sound of your wonderful name. Heaven blew every trumpet and played every horn on the wonderful, marvelous night you were born."
> ~ Nancy Tillman

We were driving. Emma Claire was three. When, out of the dang-blue yonder she asked, "Mom? How do babies get out?"

Not where do babies come from. She knows that. They are a gift from God. No. How do they get out?

"Well, pumpkin. There's a special opening."

"Where?"

"In a special place, dear. It's a special opening and it's in a special place."

Don't judge, y'all. 'Special' was the only word dancing.

And I was scared. This child never gives up. Ever. This is the same child, who, after days of frustration trying to figure out how Jesus lives in our hearts, pulled up her dress, bent her knees, pointed upward and said, "Mom? Did He come in through there?"

Finally I gave her some lame answer about how the opening is close to your knees.

I know. I'm ridiculous. I should've just told her that babies come out the same way that Jesus got in.

The reason she was asking is because she wants a baby sister. Of course she does. She already knows that babies are a gift from God and so she prays.

"God, please put a baby sister in my Mommy's tummy."

Coulter, with no emotion or concern for my well-being, interjects, "Emma Claire! Mom's too old to have a baby!"

Um, hello!

PEARL

I'm not too old to have a baby, I assured them. I was too single and too alone and too unemployed and yes, too celibate perhaps, but I was not too old.

Fast forward. Emma Claire was eight. She struck up an incredibly normal and not at all inappropriate conversation with a colleague.

"Are you divorced? I know about divorce. My parents are divorced."

"No, I've never been married."

"Oh. I thought you had to be married to have babies. My mom had a baby that died in her tummy."

Later in the car, Emma Claire goes there.

"Mom. Ms. P said that she's never been married."

"Yes."

"I don't understand. I thought you had to be married to have babies. One of her babies is white. One of her babies is black. Who's their dad?"

"Emma Claire, you don't actually have to be married to have babies. It's better if you are. God wants you to be married first."

"Well. That doesn't make sense. Ms. P didn't have a choice. Babies are a gift from God, Mom."

Yes, dear. They are.

It's not conception. It's creation. It's miraculous.

Some of us experience the miracle right there at the special opening by the knees. Some through the gift of adoption. There are black children with white parents and white children with black parents and there are American parents with Russian babies and sick parents with healthy children and single parents with multiple children and here is what I know.

We are all single mothers. Married, divorced, or widowed. The working mother, the working from home mother. The over-worked, out-of-work, forgot-to-go-to-work mother. The childless mother. The adoptive mother. The "I placed my children up for adoption" mother.

Being a single mother is the hardest job on the planet. I see this. Hear this. All the time.

At first I agreed. And then I got re-married, and it was still hard. Single mom, I've come to understand is redundant. Being a mom is a solo gig. And the best we can do is surround ourselves with family and friends, and a village of people. Our people.

And when we look into the face of our children, the children that came out of the same special opening that Jesus came into, when we look into their eyes, may we remain enchanted with the gifts with which we've been entrusted.

My time here is so limited. I feel the weight of my own self-imposed deadline, so I do what any self-respecting writer would do. I go into town and splurge on the greasiest hamburger I can find. Trip Advisor does not disappoint. When I come back, I realize what I was avoiding – writing about how it feels to be a separated momma, alone, when it's his turn to have the kids. Seriously, how did I end up here? My turn. His turn.

"We walk the planks from known to unknown and know:

He holds."

~ Ann Voskamp

DAY SIX

I was sitting. Staring. Depression hung on me like a wet blanket. Heavy.

Wet blanket. Wet sheets. You know, like when you wake up in the middle of the night and you are soaking wet and your sheets are soaking wet and you need desperately to be free because you are hot and so you stir and you kick and you cry out to the Lord to keep your beloved asleep because you've only recently started this beautiful affair and how utterly awful it would be for him to accidently touch you and think that you'd snuck out at night to go for a run.

In a sauna.

And then just like that, you're freezing. For the love, where are my blankets? My sweetheart has taken them all, and that is so rude. Doesn't he know that after my pre-menopausal night sweats, I began to freeze because the hotness has passed and then you're just — you know — wet?

No? Just me?

Okay, well for the record, I think that's where the term "wet blanket" came from.

PEARL

My kiddos were with their Dad and I was starting to waver. It's easy to be all brave and strong for a time. But it wears on you. And the daily work of bravery is exhausting.

Elisabeth Elliot says when you don't know what to do, do the next thing. Do the next right thing.

And that's where I was. One step at a time, trying to do the next.

Right.

Thing.

I missed my kids. My babies. And oh my stars, they were babies.

And I started to un-do, to re-think, to question and doubt.

Being without my children was paralyzing. Physically. Literally.

I would spend entire weekends sitting in a big leather chair, looking around, wondering what a mother's supposed to do when there are no children.

So I went to church and I heard this song about the ships from Spain, led by Cortez, and how they came to Mexico, but it was hard and not what they expected, so cries came out to go back. To go home. Not back to better, but back to known.

Cortez refused. And he ordered the ships to be burned.

Sitting in that chair, I would have entire conversations between the "I do" girl and the "I can't anymore" girl, and I would waver endlessly, and it felt like walking a balance beam or walking a plank high above ground, and I doubted the brave girl and I called her a fool, and worst of all, I doubted an all-knowing God.

Ann Voskamp says that worry is a form of atheism. It's forgetting who God is and forgetting what He has done and doubting what He can and will continue to do.

Sitting in that chair, I felt every bit the atheist.

By His grace, I finally moved from the chair. And I burned the ships. I walked the planks from known to unknown and, trusting in a Faithful God, I burned the ships.

PEARL

Walking through Eureka Springs on the way back from lunch, I couldn't help noticing the final push to elect a new president next week, as evidenced by innumerable HILLARY signs in practically every yard. I have as good a chance of winning Arkansas' electoral votes as Hillary, but it's fun to see that she'll obviously take Eureka.

It reminds me of the morning of my divorce, when my pastor showed up at my front door to do what pastors should — love on their people. My mother was mortified. This was worse than having a hole in the bootie of her pants from Play-Doh. She was still in her robe! And there was no make-up. She may have even had curlers in her hair.

Wait. That can't be right. She hasn't used curlers since the nineties, when we had to say goodbye to not only curlers, but heaven help us, bows. Mom was fifty and went several months trying to find a new hair bow when she commented to me that Dillard's no longer carried them.

There was a reason for that.

On a side note, however, I think they're coming back.

Anyway.

The pastor prayed with us and for us and then said goodbye. He texted me later. It read: "Your mother's bumper sticker scares me."

DAY SIX

My mother's bumper sticker has read *Hillary for President* since Obama won the nomination in 2008. This was 2013.

I wrote back. "Hahahahaha."

He wrote back. "I'm not kidding. It really scares me."

Do you know what I love about Jesus? That morning a staunch conservative held hands with a radical liberal and prayed for their daughter and sister in Christ, who is neither and who is both, and they could do that because they love Jesus more than they love politics.

I want my children to know that they can grow up and stand up for what they believe to be right and good and holy and they can do it with grace and compassion and side by side with those who believe just the opposite.

> "America will never be destroyed from the outside. If we falter and lose our freedoms it will be because we destroyed ourselves."
> ~ attributed to Abraham Lincoln

As I write, we are just days away from electing the next President of the United States. Bless our hearts, y'all; it's ugly.

PEARL

We've turned against each other.

It reminds me of this children's book about groundhogs fighting for the yellow fuzz of a tennis ball that has dropped into their home, and they declare war on each other. Wait. They weren't groundhogs. Dang it. What were they? Prairie dogs. Yes. And they declare war.

It's friend against friend and foe against foe, as they battle for the fuzz. In the end, they pass out from the struggle, and a dog comes back and takes it all for himself.

We've readied for battle and we've drawn lines in the sand. No, cement. We have drawn hard lines that can't easily be washed away when the tide comes in. We've declared that it's friend against friend and neighbor against neighbor and my heart hurts. And my head.

Somebody give this girl an aspirin.

We use God's name, and we cry foul at anything that doesn't resemble life as we believe it should be. And just like the alpha dog, winner takes all.

Have you ever been to a kid's science museum and they ask a volunteer to step inside a hula hoop? The leader takes the hoop from the bottom of the child to the top and a bubble closes around them. Children squeal and giggle, and it is glorious. That's the way I feel. Like I'm the volunteer and a bubble has closed in around me. Unlike the children, though, I don't want to pop it.

I want to stay inside the bubble, where maybe I won't hear stupid things and hateful things and wrong things. Maybe in the bubble I can pretend like I don't see you. Like you don't see me.

But it reminds me of Elie Wiesel and it reminds me of the Holocaust and it reminds me of what happens when we stay in the bubble.

Hiding.

Indifferent.

Remember "Don't ask, don't tell?"

That's seriously my favorite policy ever. And if I stay in my bubble and I don't ask and nobody tells me then I can pretend not to see the ugly.

It's like when someone's talking about your favorite show and you're like "Shush! I haven't seen it. I don't want to know what happened."

That's the way I feel. Somebody starts talking politics and I'm just like, "Shush! I don't want to know."

PEARL

I'm the kid who covers her ears and sings, "Lalalalalalala!"

I do see it, but I'm too small. I'm too ignorant. I'm too nobody. I'm too busy. I'm too selfish. I'm too afraid.

Yes. I am all of those things. I wish I could tell you that later this afternoon I've planned a get-out-the-vote rally, and how I'm knocking on doors and driving widows to the polling booths.

But I can't say that. Instead, I'm hiding in the hills of Northwest Arkansas where the bubble of fall leaves that surround me is glorious and safe. Plus, I've got a massage scheduled the day after I get home.

I don't have an answer. Which, dear friends, I think is the answer. The humility of not knowing.

The kind of humility that says "I don't know, and you don't know, but we are humankind and we are brothers and sisters and we can sit at the table of not-knowing and we can break bread and we can not know.

Together.

God has shown us what to do. He has told us what is good. "But what does the Lord require of us but to do justice, to love kindness, and to walk humbly with your God." ~ Micah 6:8 English Standard Version (ESV)

That. Is the answer.

When I first left my husband, my friend Jodi would say, "Yes. Yes. It's not an either-or. It's a both-and."

I pretended I understood what that meant until I finally understood what that meant.

We can be both sad and joyful. We can be both angry and forgiving. We can be both brave and scared. It can be both good and hard, and sometimes it is good because it is hard.

It's like the picture of the Native American holding up a sign that reads: The left wing and the right wing belong to the same bird.

This greatest of all democracies, America, is acting like a toddler who missed her afternoon nap. It is my way or no way, and here's the highway. It's an either-or. You are either with me or against me. You are either all, fully for everything I stand for, or you are all and fully against it.

What if it could become a both-and?

I both crazy-disagree with what you have just said, AND I still love you. What if we could BOTH do justice AND love mercy AND walk humbly with our God? What if we could remember that, while we came on different ships, we are all immigrants. We are all aliens. Longing for home. And homesick people get cranky. I know.

163

PEARL

We don't need someone telling us we have to make America great again, and we don't need someone telling us that it's already great.

We need to pop our bubbles, break away from the internet where we blast opinions and spew hate, and we need to get out and do the real business of working to heal our land.

Ya know, after my massage.

If I ever leave my bubble, I'm thinking of running for President. This is a wonderful idea. It's like the ultimate D-I-Y project. And just like all my other projects, I won't have a clue what I'm doing and I won't seek the advice of professionals, but I'll bring my village close and we'll do it together.

My campaign slogan will be this: Bless your heart, America! Pull your shit together and be nice already.

And if not me, then another mother. Seriously. If you brought together a room full of working, single moms (And let's review. We are all working single moms) we could hammer out world peace by school pick-up.

The problem is, these men have nowhere else to be. I've got an idea. Give them some lawns to mow, and invite the mommas to the table. We get shit done. And we get it done in time for carpool.

I've been thinking about what it will be like when this election is over. I've sworn off of Facebook for the final week because I'm afraid I'm not going to have any friends left.

And if I'm being honest, I don't have a lot to begin with.

Everyone says we are more divided than ever. I just think we are more lost than ever. But still. Will we have our first female President? Or will we have our first . . . never mind.

Are we more divided than ever? Flipping through my journals, I found a letter that my Aunt Ida had written to my grandparents. Again, not enough pages for the long story, but think Weezer from *Steel Magnolias* (remember, my mother is M'Lynn). And while I'd like to think I'm Shelby (but - ya know - before she dies), I'm really Trudy.

(If you haven't watched this movie, go do that right now. Seriously. I'll wait.)

PEARL

Anyway, this note from Aunt Ida falls out of my journal, and it reads:

To my Republican Friends.

The election is over. The results are known.

The will of the people has been clearly shown.

Let's forget our quarrels and show by our deeds

that we will give Ike all the help that he needs.

Let's all get together and let bitterness pass.

I'll hug your elephant and you can kiss my ____!

So. For the record, any bad words that I've used, it's totally my Aunt Ida's doing.

Aunt Ida wasn't scared of anything or anyone, save for Baptists and Republicans, and Lord have mercy on your soul if you happened to be both. But she taught me to stand up and speak out and fight for what you want, and I hope to teach my children the same.

> "Be who you are and say what you feel
> because those that mind don't matter,
> and those that matter don't mind."
> ~ Dr. Seuss

I was on the phone with my cousin Melinda. She's lived in Ohio for like forty years and she still sounds like a respectable Southerner. I've lived in the Midwest for almost half — no, wait — for exactly half my life.

Dear baby Jesus, can that be right? I was planning to stay only one, maybe two years.

Anyway, unlike Cousin Melinda, I sound like a character from the movie "Fargo" who's been living on the south side of Chicago. It's horrible. And nothing makes me madder than someone asking me why I don't have an accent. As if I'm making up the whole "I grew up in Arkansas" thing.

Even worse, when I go back home, people call me a Yankee. I don't mean to make fun of my own people, y'all. But the Yankees are in New York. I live in Nebraska.

Which makes me think of my sweet Mammaw who called Nebraska, New-braska.

Anyway.

If you're gonna make fun of my accent, you might as well get it right.

Where were we?

PEARL

Oh, yes. The phone. We were working on downloading Microsoft Word to my computer, because for whatever reason, I had purchased a fancy (read: expensive) computer and I could not — for the life of me, y'all — figure out how to type words. Like onto a document.

Teasing me for how long it had taken me to getting around to the download, Melinda said, "That's our Myra. Slow and steady."

I don't know. I've never thought of myself as slow.

And definitely not steady.

But now that we're here, it actually resonates. I mean, I am still in a state that I vowed to leave twenty years ago. So maybe, yes. A little bit slow.

I decided to look up the word "steady."

"Firm in position or place." Direct and unfaltering. Sure. I think Cousin Melinda just told me I was slow and stubborn. Yup. That actually makes more sense.

I'm thinking about Melinda because she's a lesbian. Everybody these days seems to have an opinion on lesbians. And so, since I'm an upcoming and relevant author, I want to tell you a story. A story about my lesbian cousin, Melinda. We call her Mimi.

DAY SIX

Mimi's mother, my Aunt Ida, was twenty years older than my mother, and like a Grandmother to me. She had three children, all of whom were gone from the house before I was born. My cousins were more like little sisters to my mother than like nieces.

The first memory I have of my cousin Mimi is when she tried to drown me in a garbage bin full of water. Or maybe she was trying to bathe me. Either way, I'm thinking someone should've called Social Services.

I also remember going to the gravel pit to swim. We probably almost died there too.

And I remember Hands Across America.

Hands Across America, y'all! This is exactly the kind of activity you participate in as a liberal Methodist. Singing with Michael Jackson and pretending we all had a bit of Dionne Warwick in us, we sang, "We are the world; we are the children. We are the ones who make a brighter day, so let's start giving."

There were lots of girls around that day. My cousins and their friends. Mimi drove a Volkswagen Beetle. Not a shiny new one with the perky little flower. I'm talking the real-deal Bug!

PEARL

No hit backs! (Sorry, that was for Coulter. What is it with the slug-bug, hit your mother while she's driving game?)

Mimi's Bug was filled with Coke bottles and Coke cans.

In the South, there are two drinks. Coke and Tea. With tea, you do not need to differentiate between sweet and un-sweet. It is all sweet. Saying "tea" implies sugar.

Coke, for my "pop" drinking friends, is anything that includes carbonation. Except for beer. Coke does not mean beer. Wait, does beer even have carbonation?

So that's two drinks. Coke and Tea.

When we finished holding Hands Across America, I noticed that Mimi had a can of Coke sitting on the top of her Bug, and what could be safer than a sip of your cousin's —

Holy Hell! What is that taste? (I know. Hell is not holy. I'm sorry. What is happening to me?)

I didn't even know that word in the eighties, but I knew that whatever I had just tasted needed a

Very.

Special.

Word.

Every Thanksgiving and Christmas, Mimi came home. Usually she brought a friend. I thought nothing of it. Why would I? In the late eighties, I didn't even know what a lesbian was, much less know that my cousin was one.

Mimi brought home her friend, and she lived her life, and she didn't expect anything except love in return. And from the moment she tried to kill me in a garbage tin, I have always loved Mimi.

I think I was in college before I figured it out that Mimi was a lesbian. Who am I kidding? I didn't figure it out. My sister told me.

Unfortunately, it was not the first time my sister had to reveal such shocking information. Mimi was right. I am slow.

But here's my truth. Again, just sending it out. I didn't need to know. And once I knew, I didn't need to have an opinion. In much the same way that people didn't know I was unhappy in my marriage. And when they found out, once they knew, there was really no need for an opinion.

Christians are divided on the issue of homosexuality, and I get it. I do. I have read scripture. I have studied scripture, and I understand that this is hard. But I also know that, according to scripture, I could've been stoned to death for my divorce.

PEARL

I remember sitting through a sermon once about the breakdown of the American family. This, quite obviously, is my favorite topic.

Not.

The pastor's explanation for the breakdown of the American family was homosexuality and divorce.

A different pastor, from Omaha, preached that divorce is never the right choice; that it is never the best option for our children, and anyone who said that it is, is gravely wrong.

Seriously, y'all? What Bible is he reading from? There are in fact, scriptural references, permissions as it were, for divorce. And I can assure you, I qualified.

The only way that I can see how homosexuality contributes to the breakdown of the American family is if you, not gay, were to accidentally marry a homosexual. So. Ya know, don't do that.

Sex always makes it into the top reasons listed for divorce. Do you know what destroys a married, heterosexual sex-life? Gluttony. Lovers who don't take care of themselves, and don't feel good about themselves, and it's right there in the list of sins. The ones we rush right over to get to the divorced people. And the gays.

I'm not saying we close the discussion. I'm not saying I have all the answers. I'm only offering the idea that my opinion, and yours, don't matter.

So be who God made you to be. And lay bare your heart and your soul. God's judgment alone is what matters.

For me, let love be the goal.

PEARL

Thursday, November 3, 2016

So much to say, so little time, as they say. It's the last full day of my week here at the Writers' Colony. Tomorrow, I'll rise up from my crunchy, sweaty little bed and head home.

Home. It feels like I've been away from home forever. Yet it also feels like I just arrived.

Home. Tomorrow I'll be ready, so I might as well start to clean up a bit.

Home. Ya know, this bed isn't comfortable. I'll just go ahead and launder my sheets and then I'll sleep on the couch, so that in the morning I'll be ready.

Home. While I'm thinking about it, perhaps I'll empty the dishwasher, clean out the fridge and take out the trash.

If I write for a few more hours and then hit the road, I could be home before dark.

Home. I never considered it Nebraska. Not until Mike helped me make it that way.

Yes. I'm ready to go home.

I skip my last night at the Colony. My week as a recluse is over. And in my introverted fashion, I skip town without saying goodbyes.

But I make myself a promise to one day come back.

> An excellent wife who can find?
> She is far more precious than jewels.
> The heart of her husband trusts in her,
> And he will have no lack of gain.
> ~ Proverbs 31: 10 - 11 (ESV)

On the drive home, I consider all the self-help, save-your-marriage type books I've read over the years, and it makes me want to laugh and cry. And considering that I didn't save my marriage, it makes me want a refund.

A woman's voice comes onto the radio, and I'm not really listening but I hear her say, "To learn more, visit our website at Proverbs31ministries.com.

Proverbs 31. Exactly where I should've been looking all along.

"She does him good, and not harm,
    all the days of her life.
She seeks wool and flax,
    and works with willing hands.
She is like the ships of the merchant;
    she brings her food from afar.
She rises while it is yet night
    and provides food for her household
    and portions for her maidens.
She considers a field and buys it;
    with the fruit of her hands she plants a vineyard.
She dresses herself with strength
    and makes her arms strong.
She perceives that her merchandise is profitable.
    Her lamp does not go out at night.
She puts her hands to the distaff,
    and her hands hold the spindle.
She opens her hand to the poor
    and reaches out her hands to the needy.

PEARL

She is not afraid of snow for her household,
    for all her household are clothed in scarlet.
She makes bed coverings for herself;
    her clothing is fine linen and purple.
Her husband is known in the gates
    when he sits among the elders of the land.
She makes linen garments and sells them;
    she delivers sashes to the merchant.
Strength and dignity are her clothing,
    and she laughs at the time to come.
She opens her mouth with wisdom,
    and the teaching of kindness is on her tongue.
She looks well to the ways of her household
    and does not eat the bread of idleness.
Her children rise up and call her blessed;
    her husband also, and he praises her:
'Many women have done excellently,
    but you surpass them all.'
Charm is deceitful, and beauty is vain,
    but a woman who fears the Lord is to be praised.
Give her of the fruit of her hands,
    and let her works praise her in the gates."

I am wife number three. When you share with others that you're wife number three, there's always a reaction. Like a tiny gasp of air catches in their throat.

Being a second wife is hardly news, but when you spill that your husband has not one, but two ex-wives, this is too much. This is one too many times. They look at you and pretend to not be shocked, but their eyes give them away. It's like they can't blink.

Here it is, y'all. He's only up by one. I've had one failed marriage; he's had two. I have one ex-spouse; he has two. I never considered, even for the shortest time, that I should not marry this man because he had failed twice. And me, only once.

We were just two broken people, with broken marriages, looking for someone to be broken with.

Together.

Actually that may not be true. My husband might tell you that he had no intention whatsoever of getting married again, but over time I wore him down. It took me about two months.

I fell in love with my husband's heart for the Lord.

In his early fifties, when someone introduced him to this crazy, broken, hot mess of a woman, introduced him to a woman who had felt grace, introduced him to a woman who knew a faithful and loving God, he fell in love. With me.

PEARL

So I wasn't nervous about his past; I was thankful for it. I was thankful for a flawed, broken man. He would fit together so perfectly with a flawed, broken woman.

We mistakenly believe that we must be whole before loving. And that is where we miss love. Broken pieces fit together to make a whole. You don't take two whole pieces and try to glue them back together. They are already complete.

Well, except with peanut butter, I guess. You could take two whole pieces of bread and glue them together with peanut butter, but then you'd need to add jelly or honey or maybe even a banana; but here's a thing you probably already knew. People aren't sandwiches.

When we've been broken, and we're out with the lanterns, we aren't looking for a perfect love, because we can't offer a perfect love. Only Christ can do that.

I couldn't run back to the same place that had broken me. I had to search somewhere different, because I was different.

Becoming.

And often, I felt like those around me were saying. What happened to the caterpillar? We liked her. She was quiet.

DAY SEVEN

Who is this butterfly creature, and why does she think she can fly?

And when I met a man who encouraged the flying, encouraged the dancing, encouraged the becoming —

When I met a man who only cared about my past because my wings had been bruised, but cared nothing more —

When I met a man who didn't notice that I'd put all the broken pieces back together differently, because he had never known them whole —

When I met a man who said, "Yes. That is some crazy baggage you're carrying, but here; I'll help you unpack —

Well, that's when I knew. I had found my man.

Yes. It was fast, but listen carefully, my love. When the Great God of the Universe presents you with a gift, you say "thank you."

Mike does not yet have an excellent wife, but he does consider me more precious than rubies, and he does not yet have an excellent wife, but he does have a wife who will do him good and not harm, for all of our days. No, I am not yet an excellent wife, but I will continue to dress myself with strength and make my arms strong. I will open my hands to the poor and reach out my hands to the needy.

PEARL

Hands that make strong fists hold so tightly to gifts of the Universe that we forget to let go and pass it on. And in the forgetting to share, like a river that stops flowing, we become the Dead Sea, where the gifts dry up and there is no life.

I am not yet an excellent wife, but by grace, strength and dignity will be my clothing, and I will laugh at the time to come.

I am not yet excellent, but it is my humble cry that one day my children will rise up and call me blessed; and my husband also.

As the third wife and the last wife, it is my humble prayer that in our brokenness and in our healing and in our giving thanks in all circumstances, giving thanks for the beauty from ashes, that my husband will look back on his life and say to me, "many women have done excellently, but you surpass them all."

Not because I am excellent, but because our God of all Mercies is.

DAY SEVEN

I pull into my driveway just as the sun is setting. There's no rushing in for a homecoming. My children are at their dad's house and Mike is traveling for work. But even walking into our quiet, empty home, I know that I'm experiencing my last few minutes of solitude (and selfishness, if I'm being honest) and I speak out loud, "Thank you, Lord Jesus."

PEARL

Friday, November 4, 2016

"The day will be what you make it,

so rise like the sun and burn."

~ William C. Hannan

My mother liked to make a joyful noise. Almost every morning of my childhood I'd wake to her singing, "Rise and Shine. And give God the glory. Glory."

As we got older and didn't want to wake up, she would pretend to unload the dishwasher in the nearby kitchen. The STOMP people think they invented the revolution of creating music with spoons and tubs, but I can assure you that my Mother thought of it long before.

PEARL

I often wake my children the same way. Singing the start of a new day. The time to rise and burn like the sun.

When Coulter was four, he—much like my mother in times gone by—grew tired of waiting for me to wake. So he snuck into my room, leaned next to the pillow and said, "Come on, Mom! It's time to Shine! And Rise!"

He remembered it backward, but he remembered it right. The sun doesn't rise, and then shine. It shines, always. Its light is just hidden in the darkness.

Each morning, when the sun rises, we can know and remember and give thanks that we, too, can survive the season of night; the season of darkness, and we can know that our light has come and that "the glory of the Lord is round about us." (Isaiah 60:1 ESV)

Each morning when the sun rises, we can rest in the knowledge that its flame did not extinguish during the night, and its blaze continues to shine.

And you do as well. Continue to shine. This is not a shining of sparkly jewels and shiny objects.

This shining of the sun is warm. Remember, it doesn't just shine, it also burns. And I think when we try to catch its rays and keep those rays, it gets too hot, and we get burned. The warmth is meant for spreading and the sun was meant for sharing and we don't rise to shine so that others may see us, C.S. Lewis warns; we are meant to rise and shine so that through us, others may see Him.

When I give the testimony of my life, I want people to know I have walked with our Lord.

Hot air rises. That is science. Except in our home. Except in Nebraska. Because there is no warm air during the winter, therefore it cannot rise. Even when the heat is on, I swear to you, the upstairs is flippin' cold. We defy science at our house, because that's how we roll.

Recently Coulter and I were at the Museum of Natural History and we were walking through what I suppose you could call an "evolution room," and there were skeletons of monkeys and skeletons of men, and you cannot deny the resemblance, and Coulter thought it was pretty cool, but then he hesitated and said,

"But that's not what we believe, right Mom?"

He knows that we believe in creation by a loving and omnipotent God.

I tried to explain that it's not an either-or. You don't have to believe in creation OR evolution. Clearly we have evolved. The only thing that makes me question it are politicians and ex-spouses who clearly, at times, still behave like monkeys.

Coulter was confused. I am confused. That's what faith is. Believing when you can't see. Accepting the mysterious nature of God. But to say that faith and science cannot co-exist is to miss the miracle of science altogether.

So I boiled that water down the only way I knew how.

We are spinning on this tiny round ball in the universe. A tiny round ball that scientists used to think was flat. Scientists sometimes get things right. And scientists sometimes get things wrong. Many scientists believe in something called the Big Bang Theory.

I believe that the television show "The Big Bang Theory" is flippin' hysterical. Because it bears resemblance to the truth about humanity. That scientists are flawed, because we are all flawed, and we do better when we know better, and I never want you to think you have to choose between science and faith.

I would only ask you this question, posed first to me by Pastor Doug. If the world was created with a bang, who lit the match?

I believe God spoke this world into existence. I believe He ordered the sun to shine. I do not believe that gases exploded and out came a monkey. To me, that is far more difficult to believe.

"Okay, cool. So we can look at the monkeys?"

Yes, Coulter. We can look at the monkeys.

Unfortunately, some of the monkey-ladies-turned-to-cave-men-ladies were quite busty and uncovered, and I began to rush Coulter through. He probably thought it was an anti-science thing, but it wasn't. It was the naked-cave-monkey thing. And her ginormous breasts.

I really wonder if their depiction was true. Do you think scientists know her breasts were that large, or did some man just imagine her that way? Men pay for those babies all the time.

Mike and I once got on the subject of breasts and I told him flat out —

They're tiny. There's nothin' there (which I think he had already figured out, just by looking) but I made it clear we aren't adding anything. I figured if breasts were that important, he could just visit the Museum of Natural History. Or, ya know, our local Wal-Mart.

I really don't get the whole boob thing. Unless yours tried to kill you, say, with cancer. Then I get it. Then, yes, buy

them big and glorious. Sisters, if it's something you want—
for yourself — then rise like the sun and go get those
suckers.

But, for the love of women everywhere, don't do it for your
husband. If it matters to him that much, if you aren't
beautiful in his eyes, just the way you are, then he doesn't
deserve even the ones you have.

Hmm. I didn't mean to write about breast implants.
Seriously. Where was I?

Science. The sun. Yes. Warm air rises.

That's why we must shine first. It's the shining of the sun
that radiates warmth and it's the warmth shared with
others that will cause us to shine.

Don't rise to shine.

Shine. And the rising will come.

I rise before dawn. With darkness all around me and in the
comfort of my home, I continue to write. I plan to surprise

Emma Claire at school lunch today. Surprising Coulter, of course, is out of the question. I learned quickly that sixth-graders do not appreciate public displays of momma-love or lunch-room visits.

> "I think God closes his hand around us at night.
> That's why it's dark."
> ~ Emma Claire

When Emma Claire was about five, she sat me down on the couch (the couch that just days ago we could not eat on, but having not seen anything in scripture to back me up, now allows snacks) to ask a question.

"Mom, you know how God holds us in His hands?"

"Yes."

"I think Coulter and I are next to each other."

Coulter hears her.

"Mom, why is it always His right hand? I mean, what's wrong with his left hand?"

He's sincere.

PEARL

"Let's ask Pastor about that."

And then he gives me this answer that supposedly Pastor had given him, but I think it can't possibly be right so we agreed to re-visit it.

Anyway.

"I'd never thought of it, but yes, Emma Claire. I bet y'all are next to each other."

A few days later, snuggled in tight, she brings it up again.

"Mom?"

"Yes, Emma Claire."

"You know how God holds us in His hand?"

"Uhm. Yes." Thinking how we'd quite recently covered this to the extent of my theological abilities.

"I think God closes His hand around us at night. That's why it's dark."

Seeing life, the light and the dark through the eyes of a child.

"Yes, Emma Claire. I think you're right."

It was 2013. Life was indeed dark. But from the mouth of babes, we know that He is closest when it's darkest. He hides us in the shelter of His wings. He holds us in the palm of His hand.

I imagine the pillar of fire that led the Israelites through the wilderness by night. Did it look like this cloud? Feel like this cloud? Is that what this is? Are we being led? And if so, are we being led toward the darkness? Or away?

> Drive away the shades of night
> Pierce the clouds and bring us light.
> ~ Oh Come, Oh Come Emmanuel (Author Unknown)

Hold us, Lord, but open up your hand. Pierce through the cloud. Please. And bring us light.

And suddenly I welcomed the grief. I leaned into the grief and I thought maybe, perhaps, this cloud that hovers is the Presence of our God, leading.

And His right hand? God's righteous right hand? The one that closes around us at night? Yes, those same hands were nailed to a cross and in the nailing God pierced through the cloud to bring us light.

PEARL

Suffering breeds empathy. We climb our mountains and then in turn, look back and help our brothers and sisters climb theirs.

Here is number twelve, the pearl of all pearls:

I knew nothing of suffering until I suffered. I knew nothing of grieving until I grieved. I knew nothing of love until I both suffered and grieved. Jesus suffered and His father grieved.

If we are to become more like Christ, then we "count it all as joy." (James 1:2 ESV)

We have a culture obsessed with healing. Not really healing, though. More of a "getting over it" than a true "getting better." Let's become a culture that takes our time. Let's quit pushing our people toward "Okay-ness" and let's let them be

Not.

Okay.

Let's look to nature. Watch her work. She's never in a hurry to end this one glorious season. So content with the here. The now.

DAY EIGHT

I'm watching her now, through a picture window, and her rainbow of leaves are cascading, melodically, twirling in the wind and dancing through the trees and eventually falling to the ground, where they become a big ol' crunchy mess. A big ol' crunchy, glorious mess.

This life is messy, y'all. And so is my house. And my hair. Just one big mess.

And sometimes the cup is bitter. But oh, that our Lord drank from it. He didn't let the cup pass, and when grief lands at our doorstep, neither should we.

God will meet us there. He will hide us and hold us, and you and I and Coulter and Emma Claire and all of His people will be there.

Together. In His big ol' (right!) hand.

All this talk about God's hands has begun an endless reel of "He's got the Whole World in His Hands" stuck in my head. Except I keep trying to find a rhythm where I can add "righteous right." Sometimes my dancing words sing.

PEARL

"If we had no winter,

the spring would not be so pleasant."

~ Anne Bradstreet

With all this brokenness and grief and deep Jesus-stuff, sometimes I forget to look up. And lighten up. I forget that spring has come.

I remember my fourteen year-old doctor reminding me that not everything is a crisis. For example, you don't have to freak out and become homicidal if you're running late during carpool and the driver in front of you can't figure out how to navigate a simple four-way stop. But when you've existed in crisis-mode for so long, it becomes a habit. Grief becomes a habit. You forget that it's over. That you're better.

My mom sent me an old devotional book, *Share my Pleasant Stones*, by Eugenia Price. (Don't you kind of wonder if her dad's name was Gene? And they thought they were having a boy, so at the last minute they changed it to Eugenia?)

My Pappaw's name was Reese. My cousin's name is Reesa. I always wondered if my aunt thought she was having a boy, adding the "a" when her baby girl arrived.

Kind of like Gene and Eugenia. Reese has always been one of my favorite names. When we were pregnant with Emma Claire, I wanted to name her Reese, but during the Sweet Home Alabama and Legally Blonde years, people seemed to think I had a resemblance to the actress Reese Witherspoon, and people mentioned it so often that it became hard to say, "No. No one's ever told me that."

Because they had. They did. All the time. So even though Reese was a family name, I couldn't do it. I was afraid people would think it was because I secretly wanted to be Reese Witherspoon. And then I'd spend my daughter's whole life explaining how she wasn't named after a movie star.

As it is, I've spent her whole life explaining that her name is not Emma, but Emma Claire. It's a lot like Emily. Three syllables, y'all. It's really not that difficult.

In retrospect, I really should've gone with Reese.

Where was I? Gene. Eugenia. Yes.

In this devotional, I read: "I set my heart to understand God's point, and to my amazement, I did. At first I didn't want to get it, because it meant giving up one of my most beloved symptoms."

PEARL

Feeling like everything is a crisis. Feeling that people don't like me. And if they do like me, it's only because they don't really know me.

That someone's mad at me, and if they aren't mad at me, they will be.

That someone will think I was wrong to get divorced; that I didn't hear His voice; that I didn't try hard enough, long enough, that I wasn't strong enough.

That I named my daughter after a movie star.

Life is not a crisis. I must "be willing not to feel a victim in this thing."

That is my symptom.

See how quickly I fall back into winter? See how quickly I forget spring?

That's how the words dance. That's how they twirl like the falling leaves outside my window. That's why I have to set my heart to understand God's point so that I might write this story. His story.

That I might learn, and that we might learn together, that playing the victim is a merely a symptom, and one we must be willing not to feel. Not to be.

DAY EIGHT

Speaking of four-way stops; wait, we were talking about four-way stops, right? I understand this has nothing to do with marriage and divorce and mercy and grace, but since I'm writing a book, I think Jesus will want us to talk about it.

Y'all.

It's not that hard.

There are four stops in a four-way stop. Duh. Okay, with turning lanes, maybe six. I suppose there could even be eight.

Look, even babies can count to eight. Well, at least mine did. My children are ridiculously bright, and I'm hopeful that their ACT scores will be far above the drinking age. (Which I only mention because mine wasn't.)

Recently, I overheard a young woman explaining that this election will be her first time to vote. She explained that when she turned twenty-one she had been away at college. Her friend suggested that she could've voted by absentee ballot. I suggested that she could've voted when she turned eighteen.

Lord-a-mercy, please tell me that I at least scored higher on the ACT than this girl who's confused the voting age with the drinking age!

PEARL

I recently heard an argument in favor of lowering the drinking age. This is a terrible idea. Eighteen year-olds already have the right to vote. Do we really want them drinking while they do it?

Oh wait. I forgot about college. Nobody waits for the drinking age anymore, do they? Well, that's my point, entirely. Maybe if she hadn't been so busy drinking, she'd have remembered that, in the United States, you can vote when you're eighteen.

And if Donald Trump can be elected President, you can do anything —

Never mind. No you can't.

But you can navigate four way stops. Yes. We can do this. We can do hard things. We can pull up to a stop sign, count, and wait our turn.

Mike is home! He wants me to tell him everything. My dancing words are tired. My head is tired. My body is tired. I tell him I need a vacation. He is probably thinking I just had a vacation, but he is smart enough not to say it out loud.

When I visit Emma Claire for lunch, she excitedly asks me where my book is. "It's in Mexico," I tell her.

I dive head-first back into real life and the water feels cold. I pull out my notes and wish I were back in Eureka.

I am homesick for the Writers' Colony. I was there for a week. I could stay for ten weeks more.

It is quiet there. Outside, the world stirs and there is madness. Complete madness. But there, locked away from the real world, there is only calm.

Except, what if that is the real world? What if that is what God created our hearts for?

What if the madness outside, the name-calling and cheating and clamoring and business and fullness and rushing and running; what if that is not real life at all?

What if filling our lives with more is the escape?

What if we have equated business with holiness?

I keep saying, "I took a break from real life," but that's not it. This is real. This is life. Allowing your thoughts to become sentences and hearing the meditation of your heart. Paying attention to nature and listening for the heartbeat of God.

The frantic pace of our lives, never stopping to breathe, that is the escape from real life.

If I don't pause, I don't see it. If I don't breathe, I won't hear it. If I don't stop, well, I can't stop.

Someone might see — catch — me.

We bow down to the idol of busy and we serve a "more is always better" god. But what if it's not? What if more is simply more?

The other writers at the Colony were staying far longer than I could. I gave myself one week to write this book. Y'all wanna know something? You can't write a book in just one week.

But I didn't know that.

Wednesday night, as I told my fellow writers that I'd be leaving soon, they were shocked. Already?

It reminded me of our first family ski trip. The booking agent called to get a deposit on our stay. She was confused by the idea that we were only staying two nights. Evidently, most people, after the long plow up the mountain, stay longer. We weren't. We couldn't. We were staying two days.

We also took our little ones to Disneyland, where we spent just one day. Again, evidently some people stay longer.

We do what's necessary, and then we do what's possible.

This being alone and letting words flow like from the fountain of God, is real and good and necessary.

Asked about allergies, I heard an author once respond that she was allergic to people.

Yes. I have that allergy. And the only remedy is retreat. Retreat to the patio. Retreat to the park. Sometimes, as mothers, even a few minutes behind the locked bathroom door can feel like a retreat. But my retreat to the mountains is over.

I have a husband and young children and a job and how, in all the history of the world, would my town ever survive without my leadership skills as a carpool driver?

As I said these words and the writers stared back at me, there was this look in their eyes, and oh my goodness, I saw it!

Mine is not an idol of more. It's an idol of ego. I can't stay for more than just one week, because I think I am too important. As if the people looking back at me didn't have lives, and didn't have children, and didn't have loves, and didn't have work.

Bowing down and looking up, I wondered if I could lay that idol down. As Paul Tripp puts it, "not thinking less of myself, but thinking of myself less."

We continued our dinner discussion and the writers spoke about their day. Working on mortgages and visiting with friends and going for long walks on the nearby trails.

One writer says, "Oh my God! Did you read the front page of the *New York Times* today?"

Um, no. Had I not fully explained my living-life-in-a-bubble philosophy, so that even if I wasn't hiding out in the Ozark Mountains, I wouldn't have read the *New York Times*?

I haven't watched the news since the 2008 election. Which I fully understand is nothing to brag about, but in May of 2008, four months pregnant with Emma Claire, I decided I had two choices. Yell at the crazy people on television who were quite obviously out to destroy all that is good and holy. Or stop yelling at the crazy people, stop listening to the crazy people, and simply pray for the crazy people.

I chose the latter. Primarily in hopes of not becoming one of the crazies. My children needed me sane.

Admittedly, I have taken this too far, because as I listened to them discuss the ugly election of 2016, it dawned on me I really only knew two things.

Donald Trump wants to build a wall. And I don't like walls.

All I could say to my children was that if the crazies build a wall, my prayer is that one day you'll be crazy enough to tear that motherf@#%er down!

But listening to my new friends carry on about some woman who — based on the conversation, I'm thinking is Trump's campaign manager — made some comment about Trump's dry-cleaning bill being more than most people's salary, it occurred to me.

They weren't escaping real life. They were living.

Right there. Nestled in the mountains. Living.

It probably takes a week in a place like this just to begin to feel safe and welcome the silence. They weren't locking themselves in a room to write, etching out every word possible, they were living and writing and breathing and creating.

Then again, they also had editors and publishers and, how do I say this, what's the word? Yes. Money.

Money doesn't buy happiness, but it sometimes buys time. Seriously. Again, how did I forget to pray for the money thing?

The writers continue to talk. One, totally in passing, mentioned that she'd been writing her novel for ten years.

I gently tucked my hand under my chin and tried to pretend like I was not at all surprised. Dismayed. Sympathetic.

Ten.

Holy.

Years.

Bless her heart!

Y'all. If I have to so much as walk downstairs for a glass of water while I'm writing, then I've pretty much lost whatever thought was in my head. If this book takes me ten years, I may not even be able to remember why I started writing it.

She said to me that I could take some of my essays and try to have them published, and then I wouldn't get as discouraged waiting to finish the book.

DAY EIGHT

What?

Uh, no thank you.

I'm writing this book and I only had one week, so ten years is for sure out of the question.

Seriously. Change the subject.

Retirement funds, anyone?

After divorce, when everything's been split in half and split in half again, and when retirement planning starts again at forty, well yes, when that is your story, nothing is more fun than people talking about their retirement.

Wait. Actually.

Everything is more fun.

Everything except writing the same book for ten years.

Holy anxiety.

But then I remembered a beautiful word. And it is always the words that bring me peace. His Word.

If I listen to your words, to the words and the voices around me, I get panicky and anxious and my chest gets tight and I find it hard to breathe, because again, I'm allergic. To you.

But when I remember the word that the Lord has given me, I exhale.

Almost.

That's the word I remembered.

I'm not almost fifty. I'm forty-four. I'm not almost a writer. I am a writer.

Maya Angelou says that when you know better, do better. I know now that two days of skiing is not enough. This year we've budgeted for three. I know now that one day at Disneyland is not enough. Wait. Yes, it is.

One week at the Writers' Colony this trip, this book, this time.

It's enough because it has to be. It's enough because it's what I have. But I'm a mother and a lover and I can write anywhere. My final, bonus, number thirteen pearl is this:

I don't need to escape the real world; I need to create a new one.

DAY EIGHT

The kind of world where books don't take ten years and days don't rush by unlived and children don't rush out every door. I need to create a world where we remember to be and not just almost be and we listen to hearts and we buy expensive perfume and wear treasures from the 'you must be eighteen years old to enter' store, and I don't need to be in Eureka Springs any longer.

(I have no idea where perfume came from. I don't wear perfume. It gives me a headache. And while we're on the subject, your perfume also gives me a headache.)

No, I don't need to write in the Ozark Mountains; I simply need to create a world where I see the mountains from Nebraska. Where I can hear the heartbeat of God in my own backyard. Where I can write my books and love my husband and raise my children.

I need to create a world where I don't worry about finances or deadlines or retirement funds. (Well, maybe a little bit about retirement funds.)

And when it all becomes too much; when it feels like I'm drowning; I need to remember that I can swim. I can dive for pearls. Gray pearls. That's what I found.

Not white. White is easy. So clean. So certain. My pearls are gritty and gray and beautiful.

PEARL

Save for Jesus, the Christian life is marked by uncertainty. It's in the gray. The in–between; it's within the mysteries of God that our faith takes shape.

It's in the muck and yuck and hard and the hurt. It's in divorce and adultery and loss and death and loneliness and yes, in all of this, when we can turn to our friends and we say, in this, through this, because of this — God is still good.

It's time y'all.

Dive in.

Your pearls are waiting.

And remember: Just because God created the world in seven (okay, six) days, don't think for a second that you can write a book in that amount of time. Unless you want to. Unless God tells you to, at the corner of Bell and Military. Yes, unless then.

The End

Benediction

Thank you, readers, for taking this journey with me. May the Lord be glorified in the telling and may He use my story to bless yours. And wherever you are in your story: diving, swimming, drowning, or surviving, remember that the "Lord will go before you, and the God of Israel will be your rear guard." (Isaiah 52:12b ESV)

In other words, as my Mother would say, "He's got your back!"

The Lord bless you and keep you; The Lord make his face to shine upon you and be gracious to you; the Lord lift up his countenance upon you and give you peace.

~ Numbers 6:24-26 (ESV)

211

Made in the USA
Lexington, KY
27 October 2017